The Library of Orthodox Theology

———————————

No. 1

THE PRIMACY OF PETER

THE PRIMACY OF PETER

J. MEYENDORFF

A. SCHMEMANN

N. AFANASSIEFF

N. KOULOMZINE

THE FAITH PRESS
7 TUFTON STREET LONDON SW1

FIRST PUBLISHED IN ENGLISH IN 1963

This translation © *The Faith Press, Ltd., 1963*

Translated from the French
(Editions Delachaux et Niestle Neuchâtel and Paris)

PRINTED IN GREAT BRITAIN
in 11 point Garamond type
BY THE FAITH PRESS LTD.
LEIGHTON BUZZARD

CONTENTS

*Essays 3 and 4 are translated
by Katharine Farrer*

JOHN MEYENDORFF

ST. PETER IN BYZANTINE THEOLOGY[1]

DURING the Middle Ages both the Christian West and East produced an abundant literature on St. Peter and his succession. They generally drew from the same scriptural and patristic store of texts. However, these texts, first isolated and then artificially regrouped by polemicists, can only recover their real significance if we regard them in a historical perspective and, more especially, within the framework of a consistent and well balanced ecclesiology. It is this work of 'resourcement' and integration which ecumenical thought faces to-day if it is to reach any concrete result. We will attempt here, in a brief study of the Byzantine texts concerning St. Peter, to find out whether we may discern permanent elements of an ecclesiology in the attitude of the Byzantines towards the New Testament texts on Peter, towards the tradition on the specific ministry of the 'Coryphaeus,' and finally towards the Roman conception of his succession.

In our work, we shall limit ourselves to the medieval literature subsequent to the schism between the East and the West. At first glance, such a choice of period, when the positions were already clearly formulated, might seem to be unfavourable for our purpose. Were not the minds of the writers then engaged in a sterile conflict? Were they still capable of an objective interpretation of Scripture and Tradition? Did they actually contribute to a real solution of the Petrine problem?

We will try to show that despite the inevitable exaggerations of polemical writings, our Byzantine documents authentically reflect the position of the Orthodox Church in regard to Roman ecclesiology, and have, as such, the value of a testimony very little known, often unpublished, and therefore ignored by a great number of contemporary theologians. In their attitude toward Peter and the Petrine tradition the Byzantine writers actually repeat the views of the Greek Fathers, notwithstanding the impact of contemporary problems upon their arguments. This rigid conservatism explains,

[1] In a slightly different form this study appeared in *St. Vladimir's Seminary Quarterly*, Vol. 4, 1960, No. 2–3.

to a certain extent, why the development of the Roman primacy in the West remained unnoticed for such a long time in the East. The Eastern Churches had always recognized the particular authority of Rome in ecclesiastical affairs, and at Chalcedon had emphatically acclaimed Pope Leo as a successor of Peter, a fact which did not prevent them from condemning the monothelite Pope Honorius at the Sixth Ecumenical Council in 681. Even in the ninth century they had not realized that their previous acclamations were being interpreted in Rome as formal definitions of the Roman right to a *primatus protestatis.*

The Byzantines unanimously recognized the great *authority* of the old Rome, but never understood this authority in the sense of an absolute *power.* The prestige of Rome was not due, in their eyes, only to the 'Petrine' character of this church. Indeed the famous Canon 28 of Chalcedon was for them one of the essential texts for the organization of the Church: 'It is for right reasons, that the Fathers accorded privileges to old Rome, for this city was the seat of the Emperor and Senate . . . ' The Roman authority was thus the result of both an ecclesiastical *consensus* and of those *historical realities,* which the Church fully recognized as relevant to her own life, namely, the existence of a Christian Empire. The fact of the Pope's traditional definition as the successor of Peter was by no means denied, but it was not considered as a decisive issue. In the East there were numerous 'apostolic sees': was not Jerusalem the 'mother of all the Churches'? Could not the Bishop of Antioch claim also the title of successor to Peter? These churches, however, occupied the third and the fourth rank in the hierarchy of 'privileged' churches, as established by Canon 6 of Nicaea. But the reason why the Roman Church had been accorded an incontestable precedence over all other apostolic churches was that its Petrine and Pauline 'apostolicity' was in fact added to the city's position as the capital city, and only the conjunction of both these elements gave the Bishop of Rome the right to occupy the place of a primate in the Christian world with the consensus of all the churches.[1a]

As we have said, the Christian East for a long time did not realize that in Rome this primacy of authority and influence was

---

[1a] cf. my article 'La Primauté romaine dans la tradition canonique jusqu'au concile de Chalcedoine,' in *Istina,* 1957, IV, pp. 463–82.

being progressively transformed into a more precise claim. Our task here will be to analyse the reaction of the Byzantines, when they finally understood the real nature of the problem, when they realized that the quarrel over the *Filioque* was not the only factor of opposition between the two halves of the Christian World and, moreover, that the solution of this dogmatic quarrel was impossible without a common ecclesiological criterion.

Such is the broad historical situation in which the problem of Peter was finally perceived by the Christians of the East. In their conception of the nature of primacy in the Church, the idea of 'apostolicity' played a relatively unimportant role, since in itself it did not determine the real authority of a church.[2] In the East, the *personal ministry of Peter* and the problem of his *succession* were therefore two distinct questions.

Two categories of documents present a special interest in this field: (1) texts with an exegesis of the classical scriptural passages concerning Peter, and homilies for the Feast of SS. Peter and Paul (June 29).[3] (2) Anti-Latin polemical texts. In this latter category a distinction must be made between writings of the twelfth and thirteenth centuries on one hand, and the more elaborated texts of the great theologians of the fourteenth and fifteenth on the other.

I. EXEGETES AND PREACHERS

One can safely assert that this category of Byzantine documents was not influenced at all by the schism between East and West. Greek scholars and prelates continued the tradition of the Fathers without the slightest alteration.

It would be impossible for us here to deal extensively with patristic exegeses of the various New Testament *logia* dealing with Peter.[4] We will therefore limit ourselves by referring to Origen the common teacher of the Greek fathers in the field of biblical commentary. Origen gives an extensive explanation on Matt.

---

[2] cf. the remarkable chapter on apostolicity before Chalcedon in F. Dvornik, *The Idea of Apostolicity in Byzantium and the Legend of the Apostle Andrew*, Cambridge, Mass., 1958, pp. 39–105.

[3] Numerous texts have been gathered by M. Jugie, *Theologia Dogmatica Christianorum orientalium*, Vols. I and IV.

[4] We may refer the reader to a recent and very comprehensive study of the subject by J. Ludwig, *Die Primatworte Mt, 16, 18, 19 in der altkirchlichen Exegese*, Munster, Westf., 1952.

16: 18. He rightly interprets the famous words of Christ as a consequence of the *confession* of Peter on the road of Caesarea
Philippi: Simon became the Rock on which the Church is
founded, because he expressed the true belief in the divinity of
Christ. Thus, according to Origen, all those saved by faith in Jesus
Christ receive also the keys of the Kingdom: in other words, the
successors of Peter are *all* believers. 'If we also say,' he writes,
'Thou art the Christ, the Son of the living God, then we also
become Peter (γινόμεθα Πέτρος) . . . for whoever assimilates to
Christ, becomes the Rock (Πέτρα). Does Christ give the keys of
the Kingdom to Peter alone, whereas other blessed people cannot
receive them?' [5]

This same interpretation implicitly prevails in all the patristic
texts dealing with Peter: the great Cappadocians, St. John Chrysostom and St. Augustine all concur in affirming that the *faith of Simon*
made it possible for him to become the Rock on which the Church
is founded and that in a certain sense all those who share the
same faith are his successors. This same idea is to be found in
later Byzantine writers. 'The Lord gives the keys to Peter,' says
Theophanes Kerameus, a preacher of the twelfth century, 'and
to all those who resemble him, so that the gates of the Kingdom
of heaven remain closed for the heretics, yet are easily accessible
to the faithful.' [6] In the fourteenth century, Callistus I, Patriarch
of Constantinople (1350–3, 1354–63), in a homily for the Sunday
of Orthodoxy, gives the same interpretation of the words of Christ
to Peter.[7] Other examples could easily be found.

On the other hand, a very clear patristic tradition sees the succession of Peter in the episcopal ministry. The doctrine of St. Cyprian
of Carthage on the 'See of Peter' as being present in every local
church, and not only in Rome, is well known.[8] It is also found
in the East, among people who certainly never read the *De unitate
ecclesiae* of Cyprian, but who share its main idea, thus witnessing
to it as a part of the catholic tradition of the Church. St. Gregory

---

[5] *Home. in Mat.*, XII, 10, ed. Klostermann, Leipzig, 1935 (G. C. S. 40),
pp. 85–9 (PG XIII, 997–1004).
[6] *Hom. LV*, PG CXXXII, 965 A.
[7] The homily is unpublished; its text is to be found in a manuscript of Patmos
(*Patm.* 366, fol. 412 v).
[8] cf. in particular A. d'Alès, *La théologie de St. Cyprien*, Paris, 1922,
pp. 91–218; P.-Th. Camelot, *Saint Cyprien et la Primauté*, dans *Istina*, 1957,
IV, pp. 421–34.

of Nyssa, for example, affirms that Christ 'through Peter gave to the bishops the keys of heavenly honors' [9] and the author of the *Areopagitica,* when speaking of the 'hierarchs' of the Church, refers immediately to the image of St. Peter.[10] A careful analysis of Byzantine ecclesiastical liturature, including such documents as Lives of Saints, would certainly show that this tradition is a persistent one, and indeed it belongs to the essence of Orthodox ecclesiology to consider any local bishop to be the teacher of his flock and therefore to fulfil sacramentally, through the apostolic succession, the office of the first true believer, Peter.

In the correspondence and the encyclicas of a man like St. Athanasius I, patriarch of Constantinople (1289–93, 1303–10), one can find numerous references to evangelical texts, mainly John 21, as pertaining to the episcopal office.[11] His contemporary, Patriarch John XIII (1315–19), in a letter to the emperor Andronicus II, declared that he accepted the patriarchal throne of Byzantium only after an apparition of Christ, addressing him as he once addressed the first apostle: 'If thou lovest me, Peter, feed my sheep.' [12] All this shows quite clearly that both the ecclesiastical conscience of the Byzantines and their devotion to St. Peter express the relation between the pastoral ministry of the first Apostle and the episcopal ministry in the Church.

It is therefore comprehensible why, even after the schism between East and West, Orthodox ecclesiastical writers were never ashamed of praising the 'coryphaeus' and of recognizing his preeminent function in the very foundation of the Church. They simply did not consider this praise and recognition as relevant in any way to the papal claims, since any bishop, and not only the pope, derives his ministry from the ministry of Peter.

The great Patriarch Photius is the first witness to the amazing stability in Byzantium of the traditional patristic exegesis. 'On Peter,' he writes, 'repose the foundations of the faith.' [13] 'He is

---

[9] *De castigatione,* PG, XLVI, 312 C.
[10] *De eccl. hier.,* VII, 7 PG, III, 561–4.
[11] *Letter to Andronicus,* II, *Vat. gr.* 2219, fol. 41 v; *Letters to Bishops,* ibid., fol. 122 v; *Letter to the Metropolitan of Apameia,* ibid., fol. 128; *Instructions to Bishops,* ibid., fol. 133 v, fol. 154; *Encyclica,* ibid., fol. 187 v; *Letter to the Monks of Athos,* ibid., fol. 266.
[12] Pachimeres, *De Andronico Pal.,* V, 6, ed. Bonn, II, p. 381.
[13] *Epist.* 99 *ad Niceph.,* PG, CII, 909 A.

the coryphaeus of the Apostles.' [14] Even though he betrayed Christ, 'he was not deprived of being the chief of the apostolic choir, and has been established as the rock of the Church and is proclaimed by the Truth to be keybearer of the Kingdom of heaven,' [15] One can also find expressions in which Photius aligns the foundation of the Church with the confession of Peter. 'The Lord,' he writes, 'has entrusted to Peter the keys of the Kingdom as a reward for his right confession, and on his confession he laid the foundation of the Church.' [16] Thus, for Photius, as for the later Byzantine theologians, the polemical argument artificially opposing Peter to his confession did not exist. By confessing his faith in the Divinity of the Saviour, Peter became the Rock of the Church. The Council of 879–80, which followed the reconciliation between Photius and John VIII, went even so far as to proclaim: 'The Lord placed him at the head of all Churches, saying . . . "Feed my sheep." ' [17]

Was this mere rhetoric, of which the Byzantines, to be sure, often abused? The title of 'coryphaeus,' for example, is often given not only to Peter, but also to other Apostles, especially Paul and John, and does not have a particular meaning. But it is obviously impossible to explain by rhetoric the persistence of an extremely realistic exegesis of the scriptural texts concerning Peter; the 'Coryphaeus' was held to be an essential ecclesiastical function.

Peter, Patriarch of Antioch, in a letter to Michael Cerularios, repeats, for example, the expressions of Photius when he says that 'the great Church of Christ is built on Peter.'[18] We find even more explicit texts in Theophylact of Bulgaria, who, at the beginning of the twelfth century, composed commentaries on the Gospels. Explaining Luke 22 : 32–3, he puts in the mouth of Christ the following words: 'Since I make thee the chief ($\xi\xi\alpha\rho\chi o\varsigma$) of my disciples (after this thou wilt deny me, thou wilt cry and thou wilt come back to repentance), reaffirm the others; for thus it behoves for thee to act, thou being, after me, the rock and the foundation of the Church. One must think that this was said,' continues

---

[14] *Epist. I ad Nicolaum,* PG, CII, 585 C; cf. *Hom. II on Good Friday,* in C. Mango, *The Homilies of Photius,* Cambridge, Mass., 1958, p. 59.

[15] *Hom. I,* in C. Mango, op. cit., p. 50. Almost the same expressions are used by Photius in a solemn speech delivered to the council of 867 which condemned Pope Nicholas I (*Hom. XVIII* in C. Mango, op. cit., p. 312).

[16] *Amphil,* 194, PG, CI, 933 A.

[17] Harduini, *Collectio,* VI, 232 E.

[18] PG, CXX, 800 B.

Theophylact, 'not only about the disciples who lived then, that they might recover in Peter their foundation but about all the faithful till the end of the ages. . . .' After his denial Peter 'received again, because of his repentance, the primacy over all and the presidency of the universe.' [19]

Theophylact also insists on the fact that the words of Christ in John 21 are addressed personally to Peter: 'The Lord,' he says, 'entrusts to Peter the presidency over the sheep in the world, to nobody else, but him.' [20] Elsewhere, he writes: 'If James received the throne of Jerusalem, Peter was made the teacher of the universe.' [21] In this last text one clearly discerns a conscientious theological thought, not mere rhetoric, in the distinction between the functions of James and those of Peter. We shall later see that this distinction is essential in the Byzantine conception of the Church.

The expressions of Photius and Theophylact were taken over by many others, such as Theophanes Kerameus and, in Russia, St. Cyril of Turov. Arsenius, a famous patriarch of Constantinople (1255–9, 1261–7), is also no exception to the rule, when he writes: 'He is indeed blessed, Peter, the Rock ($\Pi \acute{\epsilon} \tau \rho o \varsigma \ \tau \tilde{\eta} \varsigma \ \pi \acute{\epsilon} \tau \rho a \varsigma$) on which Christ has established the Church.' [22]

In the fourteenth century, St. Gregory Palamas is to use the same terms. Peter is the Coryphaeus, the 'first of the Apostles.' In his sermon for the Feast of June 29, Gregory goes even further and compares Peter to Adam. By giving to Simon the name of 'Peter' and by building 'on him' his Church, Christ has made him the 'father of the race of the true worshippers of God.' Like Adam, Peter was exposed to the temptation by the devil, but his fall was not a final one; he repented and was restored by Christ to the dignity of 'pastor, the supreme pastor of the whole Church.' [23] Palamas is explicit in opposing Peter to the other apostles, 'Peter,' he writes, 'belongs to the choir of the apostles, and yet is distinct from the others, because he bears a higher title.' [24] He is, indeed, their personal 'coryphaeus' and the 'foundation of the Church.' [25]

[19] *In Lucam*, PG, CXXIII, 1073 D—1076 A.
[20] *In Johannem*, PG, CXXIV, 309 A.
[21] ibid., col. 313 A.
[22] Quoted by M. Jugie, op. cit., IV, p. 328.
[23] *Hom. 28*, PG, CLI, 356–60.
[24] *Triads*, II, 1, 38, ed. Meyendorff, Louvain, 1959, p. 304.
[25] ibid., III, 1, 38, ed., cit., p. 630; cf. other references to similar passages of Palamas in our *Introduction à l'étude de Grégoire Palamas*, Paris, 1959, p. 251, note 126.

It is not difficult to present an abundance of such quotations. All Byzantine theologians, even after the conflict with Rome, speak of Peter in the same terms as Photius and Theophylact, without any attempt to attenuate the meaning of biblical texts. Their quiet assurance proves once more that they did not think of these texts as being an argument in favour of Roman ecclesiology, which they moreover ignored, and the 'logic' of which was totally alien to Eastern Christianity. The following points, however, seemed evident to them:

(1) Peter is the 'coryphaeus' of the apostolic choir; he is the first disciple of Christ and speaks always on behalf of all. It is true that other apostles, John, James and Paul, are also called 'coryphaei' and 'primates,' but Peter alone is the 'rock of the Church.' His primacy has, therefore, not only a personal character, but bears an ecclesiological significance.

(2) The words of Jesus on the road to Caesarea Philippi—'On this rock I will build my Church'—are bound to the confession of Peter. The Church exists in history because man believes in Christ, the Son of God; without this faith, there can be no Church. Peter was the first to confess this faith, and has thus become the 'head of theologians,' to use an expression of the Office of June 29; he has received the messianic title of the 'Rock,' a title which in biblical language belongs to the Messiah himself. To the extent, however, that this title depends on a man's faith, a man can also lose it. This is what happened to Peter, and he had to undergo tears of repentance before he was re-established in his dignity.

(3) The Byzantine authors consider that the words of Christ to Peter (Matt. 16: 18) possess a final and eternal significance. Peter is a mortal man, but the Church 'against which the gates of hell cannot prevail,' remains eternally founded on Peter.

2. POLEMICISTS OF THE TWELFTH TO THIRTEENTH CENTURIES

As we may easily imagine, the Byzantine anti-Latin texts are far from being all of equal value, and it is not always possible to deduce from them a consistent ecclesiology. A vast number deal with the controversy over the *Filioque,* ignoring altogether the problem of Peter and of his succession. This problem, however, became unavoidable when Byzantine theologians and prelates found them-

ST. PETER IN BYZANTINE THEOLOGY

selves face to face with the reformed and tremendously strengthened
Papacy of the twelfth century. The first serious encounter occurred
when the Emperor Manuel Comnenus initiated a policy of ecclesiastical union with the hope of recovering for himself the old
universal Roman imperial power over both East and West. Manuel
was tempted, therefore, to recognize the Western theory of the
Roman primacy as being of divine origin, but he faced the strong
opposition of Patriarch Michael of Anchialus (1170–7). Peter,
affirmed the patriarch, was a 'universal teacher,' who established
bishops not only in Rome, but also in Antioch and Jerusalem,
which have much more 'divine' reasons to become the centre of
the universal Church than does Rome; the Roman primacy was a
canonical establishment, conditioned by the orthodoxy of the
Roman bishops; after their fall into heresy, it was transferred to the
'new Rome,' Constantinople. Almost the same argument is stressed
by another Greek theologian of the period, Andronicus Camaterus.[26] It is clear, therefore, that the reaction of the Byzantine
theologians was determined by an ecclesiology which implied a
different conception of the succession of Peter.

In the period immediately following the Latin capture of Constantinople (1204), when Rome for the first time decided to
appoint bishops to oriental sees, and more particularly to Constantinople, this reaction became stronger. These appointments,
made by Innocent III, presented the Byzantines with the challenge
of Roman ecclesiology on a practical level. The Greeks could no
longer believe that the claims of Ancient Rome were not really able
to alter the old canonical procedure of episcopal election, or that
Roman centralization could not be extended beyond the limits of
the West.

Historians have more than once described the disastrous effect
of the Crusades upon the relations between Christians of East and
West. The mutual accusations turned into a real uprising of hatred
after the capture of Constantinople by the Westerners in 1204. As
is known, Innocent III began by solemnly protesting against the
violence of the Crusaders, but finally he decided to profit from the

[26] The conceptions of Michael of Anchialus are expressed in the form of a
dialogue with the emperor Manuel; the dialogue was published by Ch. Loparev
in *Vizantiiskii Vremennik*, 14 (1907), pp. 344–57. On Andronicus Camaterus,
see J. Hergenrother, *Photius, patr. von Konstantinopel*, Regensburg, 1867–9,
Vol. III, p. 813.

given situation and to act in the same way in which his predecessors had acted in other eastern territories reconquered from the Moslems. He appointed a Latin Patriarch to Constantinople. This action appeared to the whole Christian East not only as a religious sanction of the conquest, but as a sort of theological justification of aggression. The election of a Latin Emperor in Byzantium could still be interpreted as being in conformity with the laws of war, but by virtue of what right or custom was the Patriarch of the West appointing his own candidate, the Venetian Thomas Morosini, to the See of St. John Chrysostom?

In all the anti-Latin documents of that period we see mention of this so-called 'right' of the Pope, a right of which the Eastern Church had no knowledge. Thus, this action of Innocent III was the starting point of a polemic against the primacy of Rome. All of a sudden the East became aware of an ecclesiological development which had taken place in the West and which it was much too late to stop.

Several short documents, all directly connected with the appointment of Thomas Morosini, reveal to us the shock felt by the Orientals:

(1) A letter to Innocent III by the legitimate Patriarch of Constantinople John Camateros (1198–1206) who took refuge in Thrace after the fall of the capital city.[27]

(2) A treatise, sometimes wrongly attributed to Photius and entitled 'Against those who say that Rome is the first See.' [28]

(3) Two writings of the learned Deacon Nicholas Mesarites, very similar in their contents to the pseudo-Photian treatise: the first in the form of a dialogue with Morosini (a dialogue that actually took place in Constantinople on August 30, 1206),[29] the

---

[27] The letter is unpublished; it is to be found in the *Paris gr.* 1302 (thirteenth century), ff. 270ff.; cf. brief excerpts in M. Jugie, op. cit., IV, pp. 341–2.

[28] Published for the first time by Beveridge, *Synodikon sive Pandectae canonum. II*, Oxford, 1672. This document is now to be found in the critical edition of M. Gordillo, 'Photius et primatus romanus,' in *Orientalia Christiana Periodica*, VI, 1940, pp. 5–39; the editor attributes the pamphlet to a writer of the early thirteenth century. This was also the opinion of Russian scholars like Th. Kuzganov, *K izsledovaniiu o patr. Fotii, Khristianskoe Chtenie*, 1895, I, p. 198, and Th. Rossejkin, 'Vostochnyi Papism v IXm veke' in *Bogoslovskii Vestnik*, 1915, II, p. 421. The arguments recently given by F. Dvornik against the authorship of Photius can be considered as decisive (*The Photian Schism*, Cambridge, 1948, pp. 125–7, and *The Idea of Apostolicity in Byzantium*, pp. 247–53).

[29] Ed. A. Heisenberg in *Sitzungsberichte der Bayrischen Akademie der Wissenschaften, Philos., philog. und hist. Klasse*, 1923, 2. Abh.—*Neue Quellen*

second, a pamphlet written when Nicholas already became archbishop of Ephesus.[30]

(4) The letter of a patriarch of Constantinople, whose name is
unknown, to his colleague in Jerusalem.[31]

(5) An article by an unknown Greek author : 'Why has the Latin
overcome us?' attacking the appointment of Morosini with particular violence.[32]

These writings are interesting to the extent that they reflect
the first reaction of the Greek theologians to the Papacy. Their
argumentation is not always mature; for example, some of them
(Mesarites, Pseudo-Photius and the author of the anonymous
pamphlet) try, for the first time, to oppose the apostolicity of Constantinople, supposedly founded by St. Andrew, to that of Rome.
F. Dvornik has recently proved the very late origin of the legend
on which this conception is based; in any case, the argument was
quite irrelevant for the Byzantines, whose really strong and
Orthodox point against Rome was a different concept of apostolicity
itself.[33]

All the documents present arguments concerning the primacy of
Peter among the Twelve and deal with the problem of his succession. The Patriarch's letters insist especially on the first point. The
anonymous pamphlet, on the contrary, completely rejects the
primacy of Peter, an extreme position, unique, it would seem, in all
of Byzantine literature. As to Nicholas Mesarites, although he uses
as a subsidiary argument the legend of St. Andrew, he rightly bases
his main argument on the fact that the Orthodox attitude is not a
rejection of the primacy, but an interpretation of the succession
of Peter which differed from the one given by the Latins.

All the authors, with the exception of the writer of the anonymous pamphlet, call Peter 'first disciple,' 'coryphaeus' and 'rock.'

zur Geschichte der lateinischen Kaisertums und der Kirchenunion, II.—Die
unionverhandlungen von 30 Aug. 1206, Munchen, 1923.
[30] Published for the first time by archim. Arsenii in Chteniia v obshchestve
liubitelei dukhovnago prosveshcheniia, 1891 and 1893; republished by A. Heisenberg in the same Sitzungsberichte, 1923, 3. Abh., Neue Quellen, III—Der
Bericht der Nikolaos Mesarites über die politischen und kaiserlichen Ereignisse
des Jahres 1214.
[31] Ed. A. Pavlov, Kritscheskie opyty po istorii drevneishei greko-russkoi
polemiki protiv Latinjan, St. Petersburg, 1878, pp. 158–68.
[32] Ed. archim. Arsenii, Tri stat'i neizvestnago grecheskago pisatelia, Moscow,
1892, pp. 84–115.
[33] cf. F. Dvornik, The Idea of Apostolicity, pp. 289–94.

But John Camateros makes an effort to minimize the scope of these titles by opposing them to other texts of the New Testament; the Church is not founded on Peter alone, but on the 'apostles and prophets' (Eph. 2: 20); if Peter is the 'first' and the 'coryphaeus,' Paul is the 'chosen instrument' (Acts 9: 15), while James had the first place at the Council of Jerusalem. The unknown Patriarch of Constantinople, in his letter to the Patriarch of Jerusalem, goes even further in his attempt to belittle the role of Peter: 'It is impossible,' he writes, 'for a body to be deprived of its head, and for the Church to be a body without a head,' but its Head is Christ. 'The head newly introduced by the Latins not only is superfluous, but it brings confusion within the body and is a danger for it.' [34] The Romans therefore have the disease from which the church of Corinth suffered when Paul wrote to it that neither Cephas, nor Paul, or Apollos, but Christ Himself is the Head.

These arguments against the primacy of Peter, arguments which subsequent Orthodox polemicists were to make their own, give, however, no positive explanation of the role of Peter. Therefore, other parts of patriarchal letters, more ecclesiological in their tenor, are of greater importance for us.

We must first note here the essential distinction made between the function of the apostles and that of the episcopal ministry in the Church; the function of Peter, as that of the other apostles, was to be a witness for the whole world, whereas the episcopal ministry is limited to a single local church. We have already seen this distinction in the writings of Theophylact of Bulgaria. According to John Camateros, Peter is the 'universal doctor.' However, he adds, the apostolic council in Jerusalem assigned to Peter the apostolate to the circumcised, but this limitation was not a geographic one; one should not, therefore identify the function of Peter with that of the Bishop of Rome, or bind it with Rome alone.[35] The anonymous author of the anti-Latin pamphlet also insists that the apostolic function has never been limited to a specific place.[36] The point is made even clearer in the letter to the Patriarch of Jerusalem: 'Christ is the Pastor and the Master, and he has transferred the pastoral ministry to Peter. Yet we see to-day that all bishops have

[34] Ed. Pavlov, pp. 164–5.
[35] *Paris gr.* 1302, 279 B.
[36] Ed. Arsenij, pp. 107–11.

18

this very function; consequently, if Christ has accorded primacy to Peter when granting upon him the pastoral care, let this primacy be also recognized to the others, since they are pastors, and thus they will be all of them first.' [37] The unknown patriarch interprets in the same way the confession of Peter and its consequences: 'Simon has become Peter, the rock on which the church is being maintained, but others have also confessed the Divinity of Christ, and therefore are also rocks. Peter is but the first among them.' [38]

Thus the Byzantine theologians explain the New Testament texts concerning Peter within a more general ecclesiological context and more specifically in terms of a distinction between the episcopal ministry and the apostolic one. The apostles are different from the bishop in so far as the latter's function is to govern a single local church. Yet each local church has one and the same *fullness of grace;* all of them are *the Church in its totality*: the pastoral function is wholly present in every one, and all of them are established on Peter. We shall see how this point is to be developed by later Byzantine theologians; let us stress here that both John Camateros and the unknown writer of the letter to Jerusalem recognize an analogy between the primacy of Peter among the apostles and the primacy of the Bishop of Rome among the bishops.

Having recognized [writes John Camateros], a certain analogy, similar to the one found in geometry, between the relations of Peter with the other disciples of Christ, on the one hand, and the relations of the church of the Romans with the other patriarchal sees, on the other hand, we must examine whether Peter implied and held in himself the other disciples of Christ and whether the choir of the disciples was subdued to him, obeyed him as a chief and a master, leaving thus to the Roman Church a similar universal primacy. But listening to the words of the Gospel, our embarrassment is clearly dissolved.[39]

Here is the conclusion of Camateros: 'We agree to honour Peter as the first disciple of Christ, to honour him more than the others and to acclaim him as having been the head of the others; we venerate the Church of Rome as the first in rank and honour . . .

[37] Ed. Pavlov, p. 165.
[38] ibid., p. 166.
[39] *Paris gr.* 1302, ff. 271–2; quoted also in M. *Jugie,* op. cit., IV, p. 341, note 1.

but we do not see that the Scriptures oblige us to recognize in it the mother of other churches or to venerate it as embracing other churches.' [40] The unknown patriarch is approximately of the same opinion; he stresses the basic identity existing between all local churches and affirms : 'We recognize Peter as coryphaeus, in conformity with a necessary order. But Peter, not the Pope. For in the past the Pope was the first one among us, when his thought and mind were in agreement with ours. Let the identity of faith be re-established and then let him receive the primacy.' [41] In other words, the Pope is the successor of Peter only if he remains in the faith of Peter.

In the writing of Nicholas Mesarites and in the text attributed to Photius we find an identical idea, even more clearly expressed. Mesarites also distinguished the apostolate from the episcopate. He writes :

> It is true that Peter, the coryphaeus of the disciples, went to Rome; there is in this nothing sensational or extraordinary; in Rome, as in other cities, he was a doctor, not a bishop. For Linus was indeed the first bishop of Rome, elected by the holy and divine apostolic college, and then Sixtus, and, in the third place, Clement, the holy martyr, whom Peter himself has appointed to the pontifical throne. It is not true, therefore, that Peter has ever been bishop of Rome. The Italians have made the universal teacher the bishop of one city.[42]

And here is another even more explicit text :

> You try to present Peter as teacher of Rome alone. While the divine Fathers spoke of the promise made to him by the Saviour as having a *catholic* meaning and as referring to all those who believed and believe; you force yourself into a narrow and false interpretation ascribing it to Rome alone. If this were true, it would be impossible for every Church of the faithful, and not only that of Rome, to possess the Saviour properly, and for each church to be founded on the Rock, i.e. on the doctrine of Peter, in conformity with the promise.[43]

[40] *Paris gr.* 1302, fol. 272 v.
[41] Ed. Pavlov, p. 166.
[42] Ed. Heisenberg, *Neue Quellen,* II, p. 22.
[43] ibid., III, pp. 34–5.

The doctrine of the succession of Peter in Rome only seems to Mesarites a Judaic narrowing of the redeeming grace. He writes :

> If you oppose the text *Thou art Peter and on this rock I will build my church,* etc., know that this was not said about the Church of Rome. It would be Judaic and miserable to limit the grace and its divinity by lands and countries, denying to it the faculty of acting in an equal way in the whole world. When we speak of the Church One, Catholic and Apostolic, we do not mean, as does the provoking Roman ignorance, the Church of Peter or of Rome, of Byzantium or of Andrew, of Alexandria, Antioch or Palestine, we do not mean the Churches of Asia, of Europe or of Libya or the one on the northern side of the Bosphorus, but the Church which is spread in the whole universe.[44]

Leaving aside the polemic bitterness of these texts, it is clear that, faced by Roman ecclesiology, Byzantine theologians defend the ontological identity and the equality in terms of grace of all local churches. To the Roman claim to universalism, based on an institutional centre, they oppose the universalism of faith and grace. The grace of God is equally present in each Church of Christ, wherever 'two or three are gathered in His name,' i.e. wherever the Church of God exists in its sacramental and hierarchical fullness.

But then why was the Church of Rome vested with primacy among other Churches, a primacy 'analogous' to the one that Peter had among the Apostles? The Byzantines had a clear answer to this question : this Roman primacy came not from Peter, whose presence had been more effective and better attested in Jerusalem or in Antioch than in Rome, but from the fact that Rome was the capital of the Empire. Here all Byzantine authors are in agreement : the 28th Canon of Chalcedon is for them an axiom. Nicholas Mesarites concedes, it is true, that Roman primacy belongs to an old pre-Constantinian tradition, older than the Christian Empire. It had already manifested itself during the trial of Paul of Samosata : the latter's condemnation by a Council in Antioch was first communicated to Rome. According to Mesarites, this primacy was established in order to give the Bishop of Rome a greater authority in defending the interests of the Church before the pagan

---

[44] Ed. Heisenberg, *Neue Quellen,* II, p. 24; cf. Pseudo-Photius, ed. Gordillo, p. 12.

Emperors.[45] But whatever the historical inaccuracy of this scheme may be, Mesarites' essential idea is that the primacy of Rome, which was established by general consensus, is useful to the Church, but must depend on the confession of Orthodox faith.

The first reaction of the ecclesiastical consciousness in the East to the Western doctrine of primacy is therefore not an attempt to deny the primacy of Peter among the apostles, but to interpret it in terms of a concept of the Church, which differs from that which had developed in the West.

3. THE THEOLOGIANS OF FOURTEENTH AND FIFTEENTH CENTURIES

Several eminent Byzantine theologians dealt with the problem of Peter in the fourteenth and fifteenth centuries. We will limit ourselves to only four of them: Barlaam the Calabrian, Nilus Cabasilas, Symeon of Thessalonica and Gennadios Scholarios. Their thought is more elaborate and more solid than the first reaction of the Greek theologians of the thirteenth century. The argument based on the legend of St. Andrew does not appear any more.[46]

The writings of Barlaam the Calabrian, the famous adversary of St. Gregory Palamas during the Hesychast controversies, had great success in Byzantium; indeed, only his writings against Palamas were destroyed after the Council of 1341. The others, and particularly his anti-Latin treatises, were preserved and had a certain influence. Barlaam devoted three short treatises to the problem of St. Peter.[47] They are in the strict Byzantine tradition. A Greek from southern Italy, Barlaam for a long time wanted to present himself as a fervent Orthodox.

His essential argument is that the primacy of Peter is not necessarily bound to the Church of Rome. Like the authors of the thirteenth century, he makes a clear distinction between the apostolate and the episcopal ministry. 'No apostle,' he writes, 'has been appointed bishop in such or such city or land. They had everywhere the same power. As to the bishops, whom they ordained to

---

[45] Ed. Heisenberg, *Neue Quellen,* II, pp. 22–3; cf. Pseudo-Photius, ed. Gordillo, pp. 12–13.

[46] F. Dvornik, op. cit., p. 295.

[47] One of them is published in PG. CLI, 1255–80. The other two are to be found in several manuscripts (*Paris. gr.* 1278, 1218, 2751; *Vatic. gr.* 1106, 1717, 2242; *Marc. gr.* 153, etc.).

succeed them, they were pastors in various cities and countries.' [48]
Barlaam then gives an interpretation of the episcopal consecration;
if the Latins are right, he thinks, then 'Clement was established by
Peter as not only Bishop of Rome, but also as pastor of the whole
Church of God, to direct not only bishops appointed by the other
apostles, but those also whom the Coryphaeus himself appointed
in other cities. But who has ever called Peter Bishop of Rome
and Clement—Coryphaeus? Since Peter, the coryphaeus of the
apostles, has appointed many bishops in various cities, which law
obliges the Bishop of Rome alone to entitle himself the successor
of Peter and to direct the others?' [49]

Barlaam defends the ontological identity of the churches, and
consequently the equality of their bishops. Concerning the Bishop
of Rome, his conclusion is: 'The Pope has two privileges: he is
Bishop of Rome and he is first among other bishops. He has
received the Roman episcopacy from the divine Peter; as to the
primacy of honour, he was honoured with it much later by the
pious Emperors Constantine and Justinian and by divine
Councils.' [50] As bishop he is equal to the others: 'Every orthodox
bishop is the vicar of Christ and the successor of the apostles, so
that, if all the bishops of the world detach themselves from the
true faith and there remains but one guardian of the true dogmas
. . . it is in him that the faith of the divine Peter will be preserved.' [51] Moreover, the apostolic and the episcopal functions
being not identical, one cannot consider one single bishop as the
successor of one apostle. 'Bishops established by Peter are successors
not only of Peter, but also of the other apostles; just as the bishops
established by other apostles are successors of Peter.' [52]

This last point is typical of the East, where no particular signifi-

[48] PG, CLI, 1260 cD; cf. 1262 C.
[49] ibid., 1262 D—1263 C. The difference stressed here between apostles and
bishops was already clearly made by the early Fathers. St. Irenaeus of Lyons considers Linus as the first bishop of the church founded in Rome by Peter and
Paul (*Adv. Haereses*, III, 3, 3, ed. Sagnard, Paris, 1952, p. 104); the same
conception is to be found in Eusebius (*Historia ecclesiastica*, III, 2, ed. Bardy,
Paris, 1952, p. 98). The tradition according to which Clement, second or third
bishop of Rome, was also ordained by Peter goes back to Tertullian (*De
praescriptione haeritecorum*, 32, ed. Kroymann, Vienna, 1942, p. 40). It implies
that Peter ordained several consecutive bishops of Rome, but was never himself a bishop.
[50] *Paris gr.* 1278, fol. 101.
[51] ibid., fol. 127 v.
[52] ibid., fol. 130.

cance has ever been attached to the 'apostolicity' of certain local churches; were there not scores of episcopal sees pretending, often with full justification, to have been founded by the Apostles? Anyway the hierarchy of patriarchal sees was determined, not by their apostolicity, but by the authority which they were holding *de facto.* Rome held the first place only 'for the good order of the Church,' writes Barlaam.[53] And with the authors of the thirteenth century, he acknowledges a certain analogy between the apostolic choir and the episcopal college; in both cases there is one 'first' who preserves 'good order,' granting that the choice of the first bishop belongs to the Emperors and the councils.

The works of Nilus Cabasilas, an uncle of the famous Nicholas Cabasilas, who became Archbishop of Thessalonica a few months before his death, are directly dependent on the writings of Barlaam. Usually he simply repeats the expressions of the Calabrian 'philosopher' with some additional developments. Thus, he also mentions the two distinct privileges of the Pope: the Roman episcopacy and the universal primacy. Like Barlaam he sees the origin of the primacy in the *Donatio Constantini,* the 28th Canon of Chalcedon and the legislation of Justinian. But he insists, using some new terms, on the more general problem of Peter's primacy. 'Peter,' he writes, 'is at the same time apostle and chief ($\xi\xi\alpha\rho\chi o\varsigma$) of the apostles, while the Pope is neither an apostle (the apostles having ordained pastors and teachers, but not apostles) nor the Coryphaeus of the apostles. Peter is a teacher of the whole world . . . while the Pope is but the Bishop of Rome. . . . Peter ordains the Bishop of Rome, but the Pope does not nominate his successor.' [54] To some Latins who say that 'the Pope is not the bishop of a city . . . but simply bishop, being different in this from the others,' [55] Nilus answers that Orthodoxy does not know bishops that would be 'simply bishops,' the episcopal dignity being directly connected with concrete functions in a local church.

In the light of such a doctrine of the Church, Nilus interprets the words of Christ to Peter. If the Pope is the successor of Peter, inasmuch as he keeps the true faith, it is clear that the words of Christ concerning Peter no longer apply to him when he loses

[53] *Paris gr.* 1278, fol. 130.
[54] PG. CXLIX, 704 D—705 A.
[55] ibid., 701 B.

this faith. The true faith, however, can be preserved by other bishops; it is therefore obvious that the Church of Rome is not the only one built on the Rock. . . . The Church of Christ is established on the 'theology' of Peter (i.e. on his confession of Christ as God), but all those who have the true faith profess this very theology.[56] Nilus understands Matt. 16 : 18 in the manner of Origen : every true believer is a successor of Peter, but, distinct in this from the Alexandrian theologian, he accepts the full significance of the visible structures of the Church. Origenist exegesis is thus integrated into an organic and sacramental ecclesiology. The guardians of truth and the successors of Peter are for him, as for Barlaam, the heads of the churches, i.e. the bishops. Each member of the Church is, to be sure, firmly rooted on the Rock, but precisely to the extent that he belongs to the ecclesiastic organism, of which the bishop is head. 'There is nothing great in the see of Rome being called the apostolic throne, for each bishop is seated on the throne of Christ and is vested with a dignity higher than that of the angels.' [57]

In Symeon of Thessalonica, a theologian and liturgiologist of the fifteenth century, we have another witness to the Byzantine attitude towards Peter and the primacy. For him also the succession of Peter is the succession in the true faith : 'One should not contradict the Latins, when they say that the Bishop of Rome is the first. This primacy is not harmful to the Church. Let them only prove his faithfulness to the faith of Peter and to that of the successors of Peter. If it is so, let him enjoy all the privileges of Peter, let him be the first, the head, the chief of all and the supreme pontiff. . . . Let the Bishop of Rome be successor of the orthodoxy of Sylvester and Agatho, of Leo, Liberius, Martin and Gregory, then we also will call him Apostolic and the first among the other bishops; then we also will obey him, not only as Peter, but as the Saviour Himself.' [58] Evidently these words of Symeon are not a mere rhetorical exaggeration. Every Orthodox bishop, so long as he does not betray his episcopal dignity, is the image of Christ in his Church. The first among the bishops is no exception to the rule : he also is called to manifest the image of Christ in the functions

[56] PG. CXLIX, 708 B.
[57] ibid., 724 B.
[58] *Dial. contra haereses*, 23, PG, CLV, 120 AC.

which are entrusted to him, in this particular case, the primacy. It is in this sense that the *Epanagoge* of the ninth century speaks of the Patriarch of Constantinople as the 'image of Christ'; this famous text, composed probably by Photius, certainly does not contest the role of other bishops as 'images of Christ' in their own churches, but affirms that the particular function of the bishop of the capital city is to manifest this image beyond the limits of his diocese, in the life of the whole Empire.

According to Symeon, the function of primacy, which once belonged to the Bishop of Rome, has not disappeared in the Church. Within Christendom, as conceived by the Byzantines, the ancient capital city of the Empire has an intangible place, which it must recover once it returns to Orthodoxy, this being a political necessity as well as a religious one. 'By no means did we reject the Pope,' writes Symeon; 'it is not with the Pope that we refuse to enter in communion. We are bound to him, as to Christ, and we recognize him as father and shepherd. . . . In Christ, we are in communion and in an indissoluble communion with the Pope, with Peter, with Linus, with Clement. . . .' [59] But the actual Pope 'inasmuch as he is no longer their successor in the faith, is no more the inheritor of their throne.' [60] In other words, he is no longer the Pope: 'The one whom one calls Pope, will not be Pope as long as he has not the faith of Peter.' [61]

In fact Symeon expresses here a doctrine of spiritual gifts which has always been considered as obvious by Orthodox theologians. Each person can always become unworthy of the grace he has received and of the function to which the grace of the Holy Spirit has called him. His unworthiness does not suppress, however, either the gift or the function, which are essential to the life of the Church. The infallibility of the Church is therefore, in the last analysis, the faithfulness of God to His people and can never be identified with a personal infallibility, for God can force no one to be faithful to Him. Each bishop receives a charism for teaching and preserving the truth *in the Church,* in which he was made bishop. If he betrays his function he loses it, but the function remains in the Church and will be assumed by others. This is

[59] *Dial. contra haereses,* 23, PG, CLV, 121 AB.
[60] ibid., 120 D.
[61] ibid., 121 C.

exactly how Symeon of Thessalonica considers the function of primacy: it exists within the episcopal college, as it existed within the apostolic college, but it implies the unity of faith in the truth.

We find the same ecclesiological motivation expressed by the last of the great Byzantine theologians, and the first patriarch of Constantinople under Turkish dominion, Gennadios Scholarios. 'Christ established the Church on Peter,' he writes, 'as to it being invincible by the gates of hell, i.e. by impiety and heresies, he grants this invincibility to the Church, not to Peter.' [62] Peter is 'Bishop and Shepherd of the universe,' writes Scholarios, quoting the scriptural text,[63] but the same cannot be said of any of his successors, the bishops. In agreement with all the other Byzantine authors, Gennadios distinguishes between, on the one hand, the apostolic function, founded on a unique and exceptional Revelation, related to the historical event of Christ's Resurrection, and, on the other hand, the ministry of teaching entrusted within the Church to the bishops. Is not the Church 'apostolic' because it was *founded* by the apostles and can add nothing to what has been revealed once and for all to the witnesses of the Resurrection? 'The Apostles were given the wisdom and the grace from the Word which is from above and the Spirit has spoken through them . . . but once the foundation of the Church had been accomplished, it was not necessary for this grace to belong to the teachers, as once it belonged to the apostles. . . . It was necessary for the Church not to appear diminished by the absence of that grace, or for the faith to receive a lesser help from the Holy Spirit; but to the teachers, faith was sufficient, and still to-day, it is sufficient to them.' [64]

The fullness of Revelation, given in Christ, is transmitted to us by the Apostles. The Church preserves that Revelation in conformity with its own nature. A sacramental organism, it is solidly established on Peter, who confessed, on the road to Caesarea, the truth of the Incarnation. Wherever there is the fullness of this sacramental organism, there is Christ, there is the Church of God, established on Peter.

---

[62] *On the Procession of the Holy Spirit*, I, ed. Petit-Jugie, II, p. 62.
[63] *Letter to Joachim* ed. cit., IV, pp. 206–7.
[64] *On the Procession*, I, ed. cit., p. 63.

In this brief study we do not pretend that we have exhausted the content of the Byzantine writings concerning Peter. The texts that we have analysed seem sufficient, however, to state the existence of a consensus among the principal Greek theologians of the Middle Ages on some specific points.

First, it is important to note that this consensus does not concern the problem of the personal primacy of Peter among the apostles. Some of the polemicists try to deny it, while the majority simply state that the power of the keys was also given to the other apostles, and that the privilege of Peter is really a primacy and not a power essentially different from that of the other apostles. This negative statement, however, does not sufficiently explain all that the Bible means by the messianic image of the 'Petra' or the Rock, an image which Christ applies to Peter alone. The best theologians admit the personal importance of this biblical image and concentrate mainly on the problem of the *succession* of Peter. Nilus Cabasilas states clearly: 'I do not find it necessary to investigate the authority of the blessed Peter in order to know whether he was the head of the apostles and in which measure the holy apostles had to obey him. There can be here a freedom of opinion. But I affirm that it is not from Peter that the Pope got his primacy over the other bishops. The Pope has indeed two privileges: he is the Bishop of Rome . . . and he is the first among the bishops. From Peter he has received the Roman episcopacy; as to the primacy, he received it much later from the blessed Fathers and the pious Emperors, for it was just that ecclesiastical affairs be accomplished in order.' [65]

For the whole patristic tradition, accepted also by the Byzantines, the succession of Peter depends on the confession of the true faith. The confession is entrusted to each Christian at his baptism, but a particular responsibility belongs, according to the doctrine of St. Irenaeus of Lyons, to those who occupy in each local church the very throne of Christ in apostolic succession, i.e. to the bishops. The responsibility belongs *to every one* of them, since each local church has the same fullness of grace. Thus the teaching of the Byzantine theologians agrees perfectly with the ecclesiology of St. Cyprian on the 'Cathedra Petri': there is no plurality of episcopal sees, there is but one, the chair of Peter, and

[65] PG. CXLIX, 701 CD.

28

all the bishops, within the communities of which they are presidents, are seated, each one for his part, on this very chair.

Such is the essential notion of the succession of Peter in the Church in Orthodox ecclesiology. There exists, however, another succession, equally recognized by Byzantine theologians, but only on the level of the *analogy* existing between the apostolic college and the episcopal college, this second succession being determined by the need for ecclesiastical order ($\grave{\epsilon}\kappa\kappa\lambda\eta\sigma\iota\alpha\sigma\tau\iota\kappa\grave{\eta}$ $\epsilon\grave{\upsilon}\tau\alpha\xi\acute{\iota}\alpha$). Its limits are determined by the Councils, and—in the Byzantine perspective—by the 'very pious emperors.' There was a First within the apostolic college, and likewise there is a Primate among the bishops. This primacy is in a way a necessary development arising from all the measures taken by the Councils to ensure 'ecclesiastical order' : the establishment of metropolitan provinces, patriarchates, 'autocephalies,' etc. . . .

In the Orthodox perspective Roman ecclesiology appears therefore to have weighed disproportionately the 'analogous' succession of the Coryphaeus in the person of a universal primate at the expense of the succession of Peter in the person of the bishop of every local church. This lack of balance appeared little by little in history and may be explained by several historical reasons. The West can only restore this balance by a patient search of the tradition. Yet if the Orthodox are to help in this process, they must themselves initiate a careful study of their own tradition and truly become, in this particular sphere of ecclesiology, the authentic witnesses of the primitive Christian truth.

ALEXANDER SCHMEMANN

THE IDEA OF PRIMACY IN ORTHODOX ECCLESIOLOGY

I

By *primacy* we mean here an ecclesiastical power, superior to that of a bishop whose jurisdiction is limited to his diocese. In Church history and canonical tradition we find the following forms of primacy:

(a) *regional primacy*—within an ecclesiastical province or metropolitan district, i.e. in a group of dioceses (as defined, for example, in Apostolic Canon 33).

(b) primacy within the so-called *autocephalous churches*: the power of a patriarch or archbishop (e.g. the Patriarch of Moscow), and

(c) *universal primacy*: that of Rome or Constantinople.[1]

But if facts are known, their ecclesiological interpretation is virtually absent from Orthodox theology. We badly need a clarification of the nature and functions of all these primacies and, first of all, of the very concept of primacy. For both in theory and in practice there is a great deal of confusion concerning the definition of the 'supreme power' in the church, of its scope and the modes of its expression. Of the three types of primacy mentioned above, only the second—the primacy within the autocephalous church, is defined more or less precisely in each particular 'autocephaly.' But even here the ecclesiological dimension is obviously lacking and the great variety of existing patterns—from the almost absolute 'monarchy' of the Russian Patriarch to the more or less nominal primacy of the Archbishop of Athens—reveals the absence of a common understanding of primacy, or of a consistent canonical theory of it. For two hundred years Russian bishops and canonists denounced the synodal government instituted by Peter the Great as non-canonical, yet it was recognized as canonical by the

[1] For the description and canonical analysis of various forms of primacy cf. N. Zaozerskii, *The Ecclesiastical Power* (Sergiev Posad, 1894, in Russian), pp. 218ff.

other Eastern churches.[2] Why is the actual patriarchal monarchy
in Russia (the bishops even call the Patriarch their 'father') more
canonical than the collective government or the Holy Synod?
What are, in other terms, the criteria of canonicity? Obviously no
existing administrative system can be simply equated with canonical tradition. In the empirical life of the Church one administrative
system is replaced by another, and each of them is the result of a
'canonical adjustment,' i.e. the application of the canonical tradition to a particular situation. Yet, only a clear understanding of
the canonical tradition itself with all of its thelogical and ecclesiological implications can supply us with solid criteria for a canonical
evaluation of any such 'adjustments' and for measuring their
canonicity.[3]

As to the *regional* and *universal* types of primacy, there does
not exist even a *de facto* consensus of Orthodox opinion. Regional
primacy, although it is clearly sanctioned by our canonical tradition,[4] has practically disappeared from the structure and the life of
the Orthodox Churches in the triumph of centralized autocephalies.
And the idea of universal primacy is either rejected as alien to the
very spirit of Orthodoxy or formulated in terms so vague and
ambiguous that, instead of solving, they only obscure the whole
problem of primacy.[5]

And yet the solution of this problem is certainly on the agenda
for our time. It would not be difficult to prove that the canonical
and jurisdictional troubles and divisions, of which we have had too
many in the last decades, have their roots in some way or other in
this question of primacy or, to be more exact, in the absence of a

[2] Much pertaining material has been gathered in the *Opinions* of Russian
bishops, presented for the Pre-Sobor Convocation of 1906–12.
[3] cf. N. Afanassieff, 'The Permanent and the Changing Elements in Ecclesiastical Canons,' in *The Living Tradition*, Paris, 1934, pp. 82–96 (in Russian) and
also his article 'The Canons and the Canonical Consciousness' in *Put*, 1933 (in
Russian).
[4] F. Zaozerskii, op. cit., pp. 228ff.—P. V. Gidulianov, *The Metropolitan in
the First Three Centuries* (Moscow, 1905, in Russian)—N. Milash, *The Canons
of the Orthodox Church, with Commentaries* (St. Petersburg, 1911, in Russian),
Vol. 1, pp. 70ff.—H. Balsamon, *Pravoslavnaia Mysl'*, III (= *Zhivoe predanie*) in
Rhallis-Potlis, *Syntagma*, 2, 171—V. Bolotov, *Lectures in the History of Ancient
Church* (St. Petersburg, 1913, in Russian), Vol. 3, pp. 210ff.—V. Myshtzin,
The Organization of the Church in the First Two Centuries (St. Petersburg,
1909).
[5] cf. for example, the controversy aroused by the Encyclical Letter of the
Ecumenical Patriarch for the Sunday of Orthodoxy in 1950; details and
bibliography in my article 'The Ecumenical Patriarch and the Orthodox Church'
in *Tserkovnyi Vestnik*, Paris, 1951.

clearly defined doctrine of the nature and functions of primacy. And the same unsolved problem constitutes a major handicap for the unity and, therefore, the progress of Orthodoxy in countries like America where, paradoxically enough, the loyalty to a certain concept of 'canonicity' leads to the most uncanonical situation that can be imagined: the coexistence on the same territory of a number of parallel 'jurisdictions' and dioceses. . . .[6] Finally, there can be little doubt that Ecclesiology, the doctrine of the Church, is to-day at the very centre of our relations with the non-Orthodox. Among Roman Catholic theologians, there is a growing interest, and not only a 'polemical' one, in Orthodox views on Primacy; as to the Protestants, it is of vital importance that they understand our concept of the Church's universality. There are thus reasons for a genuinely theological reconsideration of the whole question. And even if no final answer can be given immediately, it will not be reached without a sustained theological effort.

2

We have defined *primacy* as a form of power. This definition, however, must be qualified at once. For there is a preliminary question: does the Orthodox Church possess a power superior to that of a bishop, i.e. a power *over* the bishop, and hence the Church of which he is the head? This question is essential for the whole problem of primacy.[7] But the answers given it by ecclesiology on the one hand, and the various ecclesiastical administrative systems on the other hand, are contradictory. Theologically and ecclesiologically the answer should be 'no': there can be no power *over* the bishop and his Church (i.e. diocese) for, 'if power belongs to the Church as one of its constituent elements, it must correspond to the nature of the Church and not be heterogeneous

---

[6] Thus it is obvious, for example, that the fatal 'jurisdictional' divisions in the Russian Church outside Russia are ultimately rooted in the question of ecclesiastical *submission* to the various 'supreme authorities,' i.e. to the problem of primacy. cf. my essays *The Church and the Ecclesiastical Structure* (Paris, 1949, in Russian)—'A Controversy on the Church' in *Tserkovnyi Vestnik*, 1950, 2—'On Neo-Papism,' ibid. 1951 (all in Russian). The development of Church life in America, on the other hand, is deeply handicapped by the absence of any connections between the ten Orthodox national jurisdictions, which for the lack of a *centre of communion* are practically isolated from each other. Here also the problem of primacy, and consequently, of an *initiative* of a 'rapprochement' is quite central.

[7] N. Afanassieff, *The Lord's Table* (Paris, 1955, in Russian)—*The Office of the Laity in the Church* (Paris, 1955, in Russian).

to it.' [8] The ministry of power and government, as all other ministries within the Church, is a *charism*, a gift of grace. It is bestowed through the sacrament of order, for only sacramentally received power is possible in the Church whose very nature is grace and whose very *institution* is based on grace. And the Church has only three charismatic orders with no gift of power superior to that of a bishop. No sacramental order of primacy, no charism of primacy exists, therefore, in the Orthodox Church; if it existed it would have a nature different from grace and, consequently, its source would not be the Church.

But in the present canonical structure of the Church such *supreme power* not only exists, but is commonly conceived as the foundation of the Church, and the basis of its canonical system.[9] Theoretically, it is true, a personal power of one bishop over another bishop is rejected; the 'supreme power' is exercised usually by the Primate together with a governing body: synod, council, etc. . . . For us, however, the important fact is that such supreme ecclesiastical government is always characterized as power over bishops, who are therefore subordinated to it. 'Supreme power' is thus introduced into the very structure of the Church as its essential element. The divorce between canonical tradition and the canonical facts is nowhere more obvious than in this universal triumph of the notion of supreme power. Having rejected and still rejecting it in its Roman form, i.e. as universal power, the Orthodox conscience has easily accepted it in the so-called 'auto-cephalies.'

In this situation the question we have formulated above cannot be answered simply by references to historical precedent or canonical texts, isolated from their context, as it is too often done in contemporary canonical controversies. We must go deeper into the very sources of Orthodox doctrine of the Church, to the essential laws of her organization and life.

3

Orthodox tradition is unanimous in its affirmation of the *Church* as an organic unity. This organism is the Body of Christ and the

---

[8] N. Afanassieff, 'The Power of Love' in *Tserkovnyi Vestnik*, 1950, 1 (22), p. 4 (in Russian).

[9] cf. for example, the Statutes of the Russian Church as adopted by the Council of 1917-18—'in the Orthodox Church of Russia the *Supreme Power* belongs to the Local Council . . .' 'The Diocese is a *part* of the Russian Church.'

C

definition is not merely symbolical but expresses the very nature of the Church.[10] It means that the visible organizational structure of the Church is the manifestation and realization of the Body of Christ or, in other terms, that this structure is rooted in the Church as the Body of Christ. But one must stress immediately that if the doctrine of the Church-Body of Christ is both scriptural and traditional, it has never really been elaborated and interpreted theologically. For reasons which cannot be discussed here (we shall mention some of them later) this doctrine disappeared rather early from canonical (i.e. ecclesiological) thinking both in the West and East, and its neglect by canonists constitutes, no doubt, a tragedy the results of which mark all domains of ecclesiastical life and thought. In the early Church the canonical tradition was an integral part of ecclesiology—of the living *experience* of the Church. But little by little it became an autonomous sphere in which the visible ecclesiastical structures, the functions of power and authority, and the relations between Churches, ceased to be explained in terms of the Church-Body of Christ. Loosing its ties with ecclesiology, the canonical tradition became 'canon law.' But in Canon Law there was no room for the notion of the Body of Christ because this notion has nothing to do with 'law.' The life of the Church came to be expressed in juridical terms, and the canons which originally were (and essentially still are) an ecclesiological testimony were transformed into, and used as, juridical norms.[11] The 'mystery of

[10] Among Russian theologians F. E. Akvilonov, *The Church: The Doctrinal definitions of the Church and the Apostolic doctrine of the Church as the Body of Christ* (St. Petersburg, 1894, in Russian)—V. Troitskii, *Essays in the History of the Doctrine of the Church* (Sergiev Posad, 1912, in Russian)—G. Florovsky, 'L'Eglise, sa nature et sa tache' in *L'Eglise Universelle dans le dessein de Dieu* (Paris, 1948). On the biblical and patristic ecclesiology cf. P. Mersch, *Le Corps Mystique du Christ, Etudes de Théologie Historique* (2 vols., Paris, 1933–6)— G. Bardy, *La Théologie de l'Eglise suivant St. Paul* (Paris, 1943)—*La Théologie de l'Eglise de St. Clément de Rome à St. Irenée* (Paris, 1945)—*La Théologie de l'Eglise de St. Irenée au Concile de Nicée* (Paris, 1947)—L. Bouyer, *L'Incarnation et l'Eglise Corps du Christ dans la théologie de St. Athanase* (Paris, 1943) —H. du Manoir, 'L'Eglise Corps du Christ, chez Cyrille d'Alexandrie' in *Dogme —et Spiritualité chez St. Cyrille d'A.* (Paris, 1944), pp. 287–366, cf. also S. Jaki, op. cit., pp. 154–203.
[11] We find in Suvorov, *The Canon Law* (Jaroslavl, 1889, in Russian) Vol. 1, p. 5, a classical expression of this juridical understanding of the Church—'The Church being a visible society cannot be outside *law.* . . . As a society, it consists of several members, linked to each other by certain relations that grow out of their life in the Church, and it also has an organization with a particular sphere of activity for each organ. . . . The regulation of relations, spheres of activities, and all the means and ways leading to the fulfilment of the Church's

the Church' was neither denied nor forgotten. It simply ceased to be understood as the only *law* of the whole life of the Church.[12]

To-day, however, an ecclesiological revival is taking place. And it is moved primarily by the desire to *express* the Church—her life, her structures, her visible unity—in adequate theological terms, and first of all in terms of the Body of Christ. It is within this revival and in connection with this 'rediscovery' of the traditional concept of the Body that new attempts are made to clarify the basic ecclesiological notions of *organism* and *organic unity*. And these, in turn, shape and condition the whole understanding of *primacy*.

The Church is an *organism*. The Church is *organic unity*. In a series of articles the contemporary Russian theologian and canonist Fr. N. Afanassieff shows that there existed (and still exist) two ecclesiological 'elaborations' or interpretations of this organic unity: the *universal* and the *eucharistic*.[13] This distinction, we shall see, is of capital importance for the understanding of the Orthodox idea of primacy.[14]

The universal ecclesiology finds its fullest expression in Roman Catholic theology, crowned by the Vatican dogma of 1870. Here the only adequate expression of the Church as organism is the universal structure of the Church, its universal unity. The Church is the *sum* of all local churches, which all together *constitute* the Body of Christ. The Church is thus conceived in terms of *whole* and *parts*. Each community, each local church is but a part, a member of this universal organism; and it participates in the Church only through its belonging to the 'whole.' In the words of one of its best exponents, Roman theology seeks a definition of the Church in which '*parts* would receive within the whole, conceived really as a whole, the status of genuine *parts*.' [15]

We do not need to go here into all details of this ecclesiology.

purpose require the *order of law.*' And since 'the means and ways' imply practically all aspects of Church life, this means that the whole life of the Church requires the order of law. Outside this order there remains only the Church as 'object of faith' (ibid., p. 6).
[12] This lack of ecclesiology in theological development has been recently stressed by G. Florovsky, op. cit., and M. J. Congar in his *Vraie et Fausse Réforme dans l'Eglise.*
[13] N. Afanassieff, 'Two Ideas of the Church Universal' in *Put.,* 1933, p. 16.
[14] N. Afanassieff, 'The Catholic Church' in *Pravoslavnaia Mysl',* 11.
[15] M. J. Congar, *Chrétiens Désunis* (Paris, 1937), p. 241; cf. also my essay 'Unity, Division, Reunion in the Light of Orthodox Ecclesiology' in *Theologia* (Athens, 1951).

The important point here is for us to see that in the light of this doctrine the need for and the reality of a universal head, i.e. the Bishop of Rome, can no longer be termed an exaggeration. It becomes not only acceptable but necessary. If the Church is a universal organism, she must have at her head a universal bishop as the focus of her unity and the organ of supreme power. The idea, popular in Orthodox apologetics, that the Church can have no visible head, because Christ is her *invisible* head, is theological nonsense.[16] If applied consistently, it should also eliminate the necessity for the *visible* head of each local church, i.e. the bishop. Yet it is the basic assumption of a 'catholic' ecclesiology that the visible structure of the Church manifests and communicates its invisible nature. The invisible Christ is made present through and in the visible unity of the bishop and the people: the Head and the Body.[17] To oppose the *visible* structure to the *invisible* Christ leads inescapably to the Protestant divorce between a visible and human Church which is contingent, relative and changing, and an invisible Church in heaven. We must simply admit that if the categories of organism and organic unity are to be applied primarily to the Church universal as the sum of all its component parts (i.e. local churches), then the one, supreme, and universal power as well as its bearer become a self-evident necessity because this unique visible organism must have a unique visible head. Thus the efforts of Roman Catholic theologians to justify Roman primacy not by mere historical contingencies but by divine institution appear as logical. Within universal ecclesiology primacy is of necessity *power* and, by the same necessity, a divinely instituted power; we have all this in a consistent form in the Roman Catholic doctrine of the Church.

4

Is this ecclesiology acceptable from the Orthodox point of view? The question may seem naive. The Orthodox Church has rejected

---

[16] Here is an example from an article, directed against the very idea of a universal centre in the Church: 'Not only the Orthodox Church has never had such a centre, but this idea completely destroys the mystery of Orthodox ecclesiology, where the Risen Christ, invisibly present, is the centre of the Church' (E. Kovalevsky, 'Ecclesiological Problem—On the articles of Fr. Sophrony and Fr. A. Schmemann' in *Vestnik Zapadno-Evzop, Ekzarkhata* (Paris, 1950), 2–3, p. 14). This argument is far from being a new one . . .

[17] Ignatius of Antioch, *Smyrn,* 8, 2.

as heretical the Roman claims and thus has implicitly condemned the ecclesiology which supports them. This answer, however, while correct in theory, is not the one which we find in facts, in the reality of life. We must remember that the rejection of Roman claims at the time of the Western Schism was due to an Orthodox 'instinct' more than to a positive ecclesiological doctrine. It was helped by violent anti-Roman feelings among the Easterners, and by the whole alienation and estrangement of the West from the East. It is well-known to-day what atmosphere of hatred, mutual suspicion and bitterness accompanied the doctrinal controversies, adding an emotional dimension,[18] to the dogmatical rupture. The rejection of Roman errors did not result in a positive elaboration of the Orthodox doctrine as was the case after the condemnation of Arianism, Nestorianism, etc. Our ecclesiology is still lacking an 'oros,' similar to the Nicean Creed in Triadology or the Chalcedon definition in Christology. But at the time of the Schism, the Church conscience both in the West and in the East was deeply affected by ideas alien to Orthodox ecclesiology. We shall deal with some of them later. Here we must stress that all of them were a denial *de facto* of the living sources of the eucharistic *ecclesiology* which constitutes, in our opinion, the basis of the true canonical tradition. I say *de facto* because the Orthodox Church, different in this respect from Rome, has never transformed this denial into a doctrine, into an ecclesiological system. Various types of 'canon law' have neither poisoned the prime sources of Church life, nor abolished or replaced the canonical tradition. Thus there is the possibility of a return to them.

What then, from the point of view which interests us in this essay, is the essence of this Orthodox ecclesiology? It is, above all, that it applies the categories of *organism* and *organic unity* to 'the Church of God abiding . . .' in every place: to the local church, to the community led by a bishop and having, in communion with him, the *fullness* of the Church. Fr. Afanassieff terms it 'eucharistic ecclesiology.' And, indeed, it is rooted in the Eucharist as the Sacrament of the Church, an Act, which ever realizes the Church as the *Body of Christ*.[19] A similar view is expressed by Fr. George

---

[18] Many details in my unpublished essay *The Unionistic Problem in the Byzantine Church*.

[19] N. Afanassieff, in *Pravoslavnaia Mysl'*, 11, pp. 21ff.

Florovsky. 'The Sacraments,' he writes, 'constitute the Church. Only in them the Christian community transcends its human dimensions and becomes the Church.' [20] Through the Eucharist we have the whole Christ and not a 'part' of Him; and therefore the Church which is 'actualized' in the Eucharist is not a 'part' or 'member' of a whole, but the Church of God in her wholeness. For it is precisely the function of the Eucharist to manifest the whole Church, her 'catholicity.' Where there is the Eucharist, there is the Church; and, conversely, only where the whole Church is (i.e. the people of God united in the Bishop, the Head, the Shepherd), there is the Eucharist. Such is the primitive ecclesiology expressed in the tradition of the early Church and still recognizable in our canons and in the liturgical 'rubrics,' which to so many seem obscure and non-essential.[21] There is no room here for the categories of the 'parts' and of the 'whole,' because it is the very essence of the sacramental-hierarchal structure that in it a 'part' not only 'agrees' with but is identical to the whole, reveals it adequately in itself, and in one word *is* the whole. The local Church as a sacramental organism, as the Gift of God in Christ, is not part or member of a wider universal organism. She is the Church. Objectively, as the Body of Christ, the Church is always identical to herself in space and time. In time, because she is always the people of God gathered to proclaim the death of the Lord and to confess His resurrection. In space, because in each local Church the fullness of gifts is given, the whole Truth is announced, the whole Christ is present, who is 'yesterday and to-day and forever the same.' In her sacramental and hierarchal order the Church reveals and conveys to men the fullness of Christ into which they must grow (cf. Eph. 4: 13).

The essential corollary of this 'eucharistic' ecclesiology is that it excludes the idea of a *supreme power,* understood as power *over* the local Church and her bishop. The ministry of power, as all

[20] G. Florovsky, op. cit., p. 65; N. Zaozerskii, op. cit., pp. 21ff.

[21] Limitations of space prevent me from dealing adequately with the connection between ecclesiology and liturgical theology; cf. my article 'Liturgical Theology: its Task and Method' in *St. Vladimir's Seminary Quarterly,* October 1957, pp. 16–27. There can be little doubt that all rubrics and rules concerning the unity of the eucharistic gathering (one Eucharist a day on the same altar by the same celebrant, etc.) have an ecclesiological significance, i.e. preserve the meaning of Eucharist as expression of the unity and fullness of the Church. Outside this ecclesiological significance they become meaningless, and as a matter of fact, are more and more frequently ignored or 'by-passed' (second altar, 'special liturgies,' etc.).

ministries and charisms, has its source in and is performed within the organic unity of the Church. It is rooted in the sacraments whose aim is to fulfil the Church as the Body of Christ. This ministry of power belongs to the bishop and there is no ministry of any higher power. A *supreme power* would mean power *over* the Church, *over* the Body of Christ, *over* Christ Himself. The bishop is vested with power, yet the root of this power is in the Church, in the Eucharistic gathering, at which he presides as priest, pastor and teacher. 'Power' in the Church can be defined and understood only within the indivisible unity of the Church, the Eucharist and the bishop. It cannot have a source different from that of the Church herself: the presence of Christ in the sacrament of the 'new eon,' of the life in the Spirit. And for the early Church all this was a living reality such that it would not be difficult to show that this reality shaped the foundations of the canonical tradition.[22] When, for example, our present and highly 'juridical' canon law affirms that all bishops are *equal in grace*, does this not mean what has been affirmed above? For what is the grace of episcopate if not the 'charism' of power? And since the Church knows of no other charism of power, there can exist no *power* higher than that of the bishop.[23]

5

Does all this mean that Orthodox ecclesiology simply rejects the very notion of *primacy*? No. But it rejects the fatal error of universal ecclesiology which identifies primacy with power, transforming the latter from a ministry in the Church into power over the Church. To explain the Orthodox conception of primacy we

[22] The basic fact for any theological interpretation of the power of the bishop (or priest) is the absolute connection between ordination and Eucharist. This connection is usually viewed as self-evident, yet it constitutes the starting point for a 'theology of power' as *power of grace*.

[23] I cannot deal here with the difficult problem of the *parish* in its relation to the diocese. Evidently, the Early Church knew only the community headed by the Bishop, who was the normal celebrant of the Eucharist, the teacher and the pastor of his church. The presbyters constituted his council—the *presbyterium*—F. J. Colson, *L'Evêque dans les communautés primitives* (Paris, 1951)—H. Chirat, *L'Assemblée Chrétienne à l'âge apostolique* (Paris, 1949) and symposium *Etudes sur le Sacrament de l'Ordre* (Paris, 1957). The division of the diocese into parishes and the corresponding transformation of the presbyter into a parish rector came later, and this change has never been seriously studied and interpreted theologically. In any case it cannot contradict the basic principles of Eucharistic ecclesiology, for it would then contradict the nature of the Church.

must now consider the approach of eucharistic ecclesiology towards the Church universal. It must be stated emphatically that this type of ecclesiology does not transform the local Church into a self-sufficient monad, without any 'organic' link with other similar monads. There is no 'congregationalism' here.[24] The organic unity of the Church universal is not less real than the organic unity of the local Church. But if universal ecclesiology interprets it in terms of 'parts' and 'whole,' for eucharistic ecclesiology the adequate term is that of *identity*: 'the Church of God abiding in . . .' The Church of God is the one and indivisible Body of Christ, wholly and indivisibly present in each Church, i.e. in the visible unity of the people of God, the Bishop and the Eucharist. And if universal unity is indeed *unity of the Church* and not merely *unity of Churches,* its essence is not that all churches together constitute one vast, unique organism, but that each Church—in the identity of order, faith and the gifts of the Holy Spirit—is the *same* Church, the same Body of Christ, indivisibly present wherever is the 'ecclesia.' It is thus the same organic unity of the church herself, the 'Churches' being not complementary to each other, as parts or members, but each one and all of them together being nothing else, but the One, Holy, Catholic, and Apostolic Church.

It is this ontological identity of all Churches with the Church of God that establish the connecting link between Churches, making them the Church universal. For the fullness (pleroma) of each local Church not only does not contradict her *need* for other Churches and, indeed, her *dependence* on them, but implies them as her own *conditio sine qua non.* On the one hand the fullness of each local Church is the same that is given to every other Church; it is a fullness possessed in common as the gift of God. And on the other hand, she has it *only* in agreement with all other churches, and only inasmuch as she does not separate herself from this agreement, does not make the one and indivisible gift her own, 'private' gift. . . .

'A new bishop shall be installed by all bishops of the province. . . .'

In this Canon 4 of the Council of Nicaea—which simply sanctions

---

[24] cf. the already mentioned articles of E. Kovalevsky and also Hierom. Sophrony, 'The Unity of the Church in the Image of Trinity' in *Vestnik Zapadno-Evzop, Ekzarkhata* (Paris, 1950), 2–3, pp. 8–33.

an already existing practice (cf. Hippolytus' Apostolic Tradition)—
we find the first and the most comprehensive form of the *inter-
dependence* of several churches. The local Church receives the condition and the 'note' of her fullness—the episcopate—through the
bishops of other Churches. What is the meaning of this dependence? The universal—'whole-and-parts'—ecclesiology uses this
canon as its main justification and proof : the plurality of the consecrators signifies the 'whole' to which the local church—the 'part'
—is therefore subordinated.[25] Such interpretation could appear
only at a time when the real link between the bishop and his Church
was forgotten and the charism of episcopacy had come to be
thought of as a personal gift which any 'two or three' bishops
could bestow on any one, and when 'valid consecration' became the
only content of the notion of apostolic succession. The meaning of
this canon appears quite different if we look into the early practice
of the Church as described, for example, in the 'Apostolic Tradition' of Hippolytus. The consecration of a bishop is followed by
the Eucharist which is offered by the newly consecrated bishop and
not by any of the consecrators.[26] This seemingly minor 'liturgical'
detail expresses in fact an important norm of the primitive ecclesiology. From the moment he is elected and consecrated, the bishop
is the president of the Eucharistic assembly, i.e. the head of the
Church, and his consecration finds its fulfilment when for the
first time he offers to God the Eucharist of the Church. Thus the
consecration of a bishop is first of all the *testimony* that this man,
elected by his own Church, is elected and appointed by God, and
that through his election and consecration his Church is identical
with the Church of God which abides in all Churches. . . .[27] It is
not the transfer of a gift by those who possess it, but the manifestation of the fact that the *same* gift, which they have received in the
Church from God, has now been given to this bishop in this
Church. Episcopate is not a 'collective gift' which any 'two or three'
bishops can convey to another man, but a ministry in the Church,
a gift given to the Church; therefore the 'cheirotonia' of a bishop
bears testimony that the Church *has* received it. The unbroken

---

[25] N. Milash, op. cit., pp. 46–7; cf. Dom. B. Botte, 'L'Ordre d'apres les
prieres d'ordination' in *Le Sacrament de l'ordre*, p. 31.
[26] Hippolytus of Rome, *Apost. Tradition*, I, 4.
[27] On the notion of *witness* in sacraments of N. Afanassieff, 'Sacramenta
et Sacramentalia' in *Pravoslavnaia Mysl'*, 10.

Episcopal succession, which was the decisive argument in the polemics against gnosticism, was understood primarily as the succession of bishops within 'every Church and not in terms of 'consecrators.'[28] To-day, however, the emphasis in the doctrine of Apostolic succession has shifted to the question of consecrators. But such was not the meaning given this doctrine by St. Irenaeus[29]; for in spite of the fact that no bishop could be consecrated by his predecessor in the same chair, it is precisely this succession in the chair which is all important to St. Irenaeus and is to him the proof of the 'identity' of the Church in time and space with the Church of God, with the fullness of Christ's gift—for 'the Church is in the bishop and the bishop is in the Church.' The consecration of a bishop by other bishops is thus the acknowledgment of the will of God as being fulfilled in this particular Church. This fulfilment includes, to be sure, the bestowing of the charism of the Holy Spirit upon the candidate, and from this point of view the consecrators are *the* ministers of the sacrament of Order. But this they are because of their function and ministry in the Church and not in virtue of a power over grace, inherent to their 'rank.' Sacramental theology has dealt almost exclusively with the *right* of the bishops to consecrate other bishops but has badly neglected the ecclesiological *content* and meaning of this right, which come precisely from the bishop's function as *witness* of God's will in the Church, his 'charism' being to keep the Church in the will of God and guide her towards its fulfilment. The Church whose bishop has died has also lost the power to express this testimony. The testimony, therefore, must of necessity come from other Churches and through their ministers who have the charism of proclaiming the will of God. In other terms, this aspect of *testimony* (the absence of which may lead eventually to an almost magical understanding of the sacrament of order) is essential to the consecration; while the gift of the Spirit comes not *from* the bishops, yet their presence, unity and testimony are the signs of its having been given to this particular Church by God Himself; they are indeed the 'form' of the sacrament.[30]

[28] J. Meyendorff in *Dieu Vivant*, 26, 1954.
[29] cf. Iren. of Lyons, *Adv. Haer.* IV, III, 3, and G. Bardy, *La Théologie de l'Eglise de St. Clément de Rome à St. Irenée*, pp. 183ff. On *diadoche* in Irenaeus cf. E. Caspar, *Die älteste Romische Bischofliste* (Berlin, 1926), p. 444.
[30] For this reason both *election* and *ordination* are essential and necessary elements in the Orthodox rite of the appointment of bishops.

The dependence of each Church on other Churches is thus a dependence not of submission but of testimony: each Church testifying about all others and all together testifying about each that they are *one* in faith and life and that separately and all together they are the Church of God—the indivisible gift of the new life in Christ. Each Church has fullness in herself, acknowledged and fulfilled in the unity of the bishop and the people; and it is the identity of this fullness with the fullness of the Church of God (and, therefore, with the 'pleroma' of every other Church) that is both expressed and maintained in the consecration of a new bishop by other bishops. Thus the organic unity of the Church as Body of Christ does not divide her into 'parts' nor make the life of any local Church 'partial'; it prevents the isolation of the local Church into a self-sufficient organism with no need for other Churches. And we should add that the conscience of the universal unity of the Church, of living koinonia and mutual responsibility and the joy of belonging to the one household of God, has never been stronger than during the short triumph of precisely this type of ecclesiology.[31]

6

The sacrament of episcopal consecration reveals the first and the essential form of *primacy,* or rather the basis of primacy: the *Synod of bishops.* In Orthodoxy the Synod is usually given an exceptional importance. The Church is often described as the Church of the Councils and her government as 'conciliary' ('sobornyi' in Russian). But very little has been done to define the nature and function of synods in theological terms. Canonically the Synod is interpreted as the 'supreme authority' in the Church. Such, we have seen, is the inescapable logic of canon law once it has ceased to be governed internally by the doctrine of the Church as Body of Christ. In fact, to the Roman doctrine of a *personal* supreme power one opposed, on the Orthodox side, the theory of a collective supreme power; and in contemporary controversies the only question debated is that of the *limits* of such a 'college'— whether it should consist of bishops only or include 'representatives' from clergy and laity. This theory acquired a new vitality after it was combined—in a rather inconsistent way—with the Slavophile

---

[31] Iren. of Lyons, *Adv. Haer.*—III, XXIV, 1.

teaching about the 'sobornost,' and this combination made it possible to accuse Roman Catholicism with a clear conscience of being overjuridical in its ecclesiology.

However, the idea of Synod as 'the visible supreme constitutive and governing organ of Church power' [32] does not correspond either to the Slavophile doctrine of 'Sobornost' [33] or to the original function of the Synod in the Church. The Synod is not 'power' in the juridical sense of this word, for there can exist no power over the Church Body of Christ. The Synod is, rather, a *witness* to the identity of all Churches as the Church of God in faith, life and 'agape.' If in his own Church the Bishop is priest, teacher and pastor, the divinely appointed witness and keeper of the catholic faith, it is through the agreement of all bishops, as revealed in the Synod, that all Churches both manifest and maintain the ontological unity of Tradition, 'for languages differ in the world, but the force of Tradition is the same' (St. Irenaeus). The Synod of Bishops is not an organ of power over the Church, nor is it 'greater' or 'fuller' than the fullness of any local Church, but in and through it all Churches acknowledge and realize their ontological unity as the One, Holy, Catholic and Apostolic Church.

Ecclesiologically and dogmatically the Synod is *necessary* for the consecration of a bishop. The sacrament of order is its ecclesiological foundation [34] because, as we have seen, the Synod is the essential condition of the fullness of each local Church, of her 'pleroma' as Body of Christ. But it also has another equally important function. The Church which by her very nature belongs to the new eon, to the Kingdom of the age to come, yet abides in history, in time, in 'this world.' She is in *statu patriae,* but also in *statu viae.* She is Fullness, but she is also Mission : the Divine love, the Divine will of salvation addressed to the world. And it is by being Mission, by loving those for whom Christ died, that the Church realizes herself as the Fullness. A Church that would isolate herself from the world and live by her eschatological fullness, that would cease to 'evangelize,' to bear witness to Christ in the world,

---

[32] N. Zaozerskii, op. cit., p. 223.

[33] cf. A. Khomiakov, 'Letter to the Editor of L'Union Chrétienne' in *Complete Works,* 1860, t. 2, pp. 30ff.

[34] G. Florovsky, 'The Sacrament of Pentecost' (A Russian View on Apostolic Succession) in *The Journal of the Fellowship of St. Alban and St. Sergius.* March 1934, N 23, pp. 29–34.

would simply cease to be the Church—because the fullness by which she lives is precisely the agape of God as revealed and communicated in Christ. 'Mission' cannot, therefore, be a static relationship with the world. It means fight with, and for, the world; it means a constant effort to understand and to challenge, to question and to answer. And this means finally that within the Church herself there must constantly arise doubts and problems and the need for a fresh renewal of the living testimony. The 'world,' both outside and inside the Church, tempts and challenges her with all its powers of destruction and doubt, idolatry and sin. This challenge calls for a common effort of all churches, for a faithful and living 'koinonia' and agreement. It is this mission of the Church in the world, her 'working' in time and history, that give the Synod its second function : to be the *common voice,* the common testimony of several (or all) Churches in their ontological unity. Thus the Apostolic Synod meets not as a regular and necessary 'organ' of the Church, but in connection with a problem arising out of the missionary situation in the Church. There is no evidence for any Synod of this type till the end of the second century when Montanism provoked a common resistance of the ecclesiastical body.[35] In the third century the African Synod appears as a regular institution, but again its regularity is not that of an organ of power, but that of orderly consultations on common problems. Finally the council of Nicaea and all subsequent Ecumenical Councils always convened to confront a problem which was vital to all Churches and which required their common testimony. It is the *truth* of its decision and not any 'constitutional right or guarantee' that makes it the highest authority in the Church.

7

It is in the Synod that *primacy* finds its first and most general expression. The Synod, since its basic purpose is the consecration of a bishop, is primarily a *regional* Synod, i.e. the council of a definite geographical area. The boundaries of such an area can be fixed in various ways : they can be geographical or coincide with a political administrative unit or be the limits of Christian expansion from an ecclesiastical centre : in Church history there is ample

---

[35] A. Pokrovskii, *The Synods of the Early Church* (Sergiev Posad, 1914, in Russian).

evidence for all of these systems. But ecclesiastically the essential feature of a *district* is the participation of all its bishops in the consecration of a new bishop (cf. Canon 4 of Nicaea). And its second constitutive element is the existence among these bishops of a clearly defined primacy of the *first bishop*. This primacy is defined in the famous Apostolic Canon 34: 'The bishops of every nation must acknowledge him who is first among them and account him as their head, and do nothing of consequence without his consent . . . but neither let him (who is the first) do anything without the consent of all; for so there will be unanimity . . .'

Here the essence of the regional primacy is stated quite clearly: it is not 'power' or 'jurisdiction' (for the primate can do nothing without the assent of all), but the expression of the unity and unanimity of all bishops and, consequently, of all Churches of the area.

There is no need to go into all the details of the rather complicated history of the *metropolitan district* in the ancient Church.[36] There can be little doubt that it was the most common, the most natural and basic form of relationship between local Churches, the basic link of their unity, rooted in the sacrament of order. There can also be little doubt that for a long time the *local primacy* was universally understood and accepted as the basic expression of the very function of primacy. To use modern terminology each 'metropolitan district' was 'autocephalous' (this is confirmed by Balsamon), since the main principle of 'autocephaly' is precisely the right to elect and consecrate new bishops.

But local primacy is not the only form of primacy to be found in our canonical tradition. Almost from the very beginning there existed also wider groupings of Churches with a corresponding 'centre of agreement' or primacy within them. One can argue which form of primacy appeared first. For, as it is well known, Christianity was settled first in the major cities of the Roman Empire and from there spread into the suburban areas. And since a metropolitan district implies the existence of a number of Churches in a given area, it is only natural to think that at first the function of primacy belonged exclusively to the Churches of the great metropolitan centres. Even after the growth in number of local churches

---

[36] V. Bolotov, op. cit., t. 3.

and the consequent shaping of metropolitan districts, the original 'centres' or 'mother-churches' did not lose their special status, their particular primacy. One could call this later stage 'second degree primacy.' In the second and third centuries such was the position of Rome, Antioch, Alexandria, Lyons, Carthage, etc. What then were the nature and the functions of this form of primacy? The well known Canon 6 of Nicaea applies to it the term *power* (exousia). But Bishop N. Milash in his commentary of this canon shows quite clearly that 'power' here must be understood as 'priority' or 'privilege.'[37] The canon defines the relationship between the Bishop of Alexandria and the four metropolitans of the Diocese of Egypt. In Egypt the metropolitan system appeared later than elsewhere and the Bishop of Alexandria, who was from the beginning the 'head' of the whole Egyptian Church (i.e. the Primate of all bishops), had, therefore, the privilege of primacy everywhere (i.e. the right to convene the Synods for the consecration of new bishops). The Council of Nicaea, which sanctioned the metropolitan system, had to establish for Egypt a kind of synthesis between the universal norm and the local particularities. On the one hand, it emphasized that no bishop could be consecrated without the assent of the metropolitan (thereby affirming the 'local primacy') but, on the other hand, it left with the Bishop of Alexandria the ultimate approval of all elections. But, as a general rule, this latter form of primacy was defined in Nicaea as *priority*, and history shows clearly enough the nature of that priority: one can describe it as *primacy of authority*. Let us stress that we have here not so much the primacy of a bishop (as in the case of the metropolitan district) but the primacy of a particular church, her special spiritual and doctrinal authority among other Churches. The great majority of local Christian communities was born from the missionary activity of some important urban Church. From the latter they received the rule of faith, the rule of prayer and the 'apostolic succession.' Many of these great Churches had, in addition, Apostles or their first disciples for founders. Furthermore they were usually better equipped theologically and intellectually. It is natural, then, that in difficult or controversial cases, these Churches took upon themselves the initi-

[37] N. Milash, op. cit., v. I, pp. 194–204—To E. R. Hardy this canon indicates that the Bishop of Alexandria was *de facto* Metropolitan of the whole of Egypt; cf. *Christian Egypt Church and People* (New York, 1952), pp. 54–9

ative of appeasement or, in other terms, of reaching and expressing the 'agreement' of all churches. The local Churches looked to them for guidance and counsel and recognized in their voice a special authority. We have early examples of such authority in the activity of St. Ignatius of Antioch, St. Polycarp of Smyrna, St. Irenaeus of Lyons, and later, in the councils of Antioch and Carthage. Yet primacy of authority here cannot be defined in juridical norms, because it has nothing to do with *'jus'* as such; yet it was quite real in the life of the early Church and the seeds of the future patriarchates are to be found in it. Once again we must stress that its essence and purpose is not 'power,' but the manifestation of the existent unity of the Churches in faith and life.

Finally we come to the highest and ultimate form of primacy: *the universal primacy.* An age-long anti-Roman prejudice has led some Orthodox canonists simply to deny the existence of such primacy in the past or the need for it in the present. But an objective study of the canonical tradition cannot fail to establish beyond any doubt that, along with local 'centres of agreement' or primacies, the Church had also known a universal primacy. The ecclesiological error of Rome lies not in the affirmation of her universal primacy. Rather, the error lies in the identification of this primacy with 'supreme power' which transforms Rome into the *principium radix et origio* [38] of the unity of the Church and of the Church herself. This ecclesiological distortion, however, must not force us into a simple rejection of universal primacy. On the contrary it ought to encourage its genuinely Orthodox interpretation.

It is impossible to deny that even before the appearance of local primacies the Church from the first days of the existence possessed an ecumenical centre of her unity and agreement. In the Apostolic and the Judaeo-Christian period it was the Church of Jerusalem, and later the Church of Rome—'presiding in agape' according to St. Ignatius of Antioch. This formula and the definition of the universal primacy contained in it have been aptly analysed by Fr. Afanassieff and we need not repeat here his argument.[39] Neither can we quote here all the testimonies of the Fathers and Councils unanimously acknowledging Rome as the senior Church and the

---

[38] 'Encycl. S. Offic. Ad Episcopos Angliae, 16 Sept., 1864' in *Denzinger Banwart,* ed. 10, n. 1686.
[39] 'The Catholic Church' in *Pravoslavnaia Mysl',* 11.

centre of ecumenical agreement.[40] It is only for the sake of biased polemics that one can ignore these testimonies, their consensus and significance. It has happened, however, that if Roman historians and theologians have always interpreted this evidence *in juridical* terms, thus falsifying its real meaning, their Orthodox opponents have systematically belittled the evidence itself. Orthodox theology is still awaiting a truly Orthodox evaluation of universal primacy in the first millennium of Church history—an evaluation free from polemical or apologetic exaggerations. Such study will certainly reveal that the essence and purpose of this primacy is to express and preserve the unity of the Church in faith and life; to express and preserve the unanimity of all Churches; to keep them from isolating themselves into ecclesiastical provincialism, loosing the Catholic ties, separating themselves from the unity of life. It means ultimately to assume the care, the *sollicitudo*[41] of the Churches so that each one of them can abide in that fullness which is always the *whole* catholic tradition and not any 'part' of it.

From this brief analysis of the concept of primacy we can draw the following general conclusion: primacy in the Church is not 'supreme power,' this notion being incompatible with the nature of the Church as Body of Christ. But neither is primacy a mere 'chairmanship' if one understands this term in its modern, parliamentary and democratic connotations. It has its roots, as all other functions, in the Church—Body of Christ. In each Church there fully abides and is always 'actualized' the Church of God; yet all together the Churches are still the same one and indivisible Church of God, the Body of Christ. The Church of God is manifested in the plurality of the Churches; but because ontologically they are the *same* Church, this ontological identity is expressed in a visible, living, and constantly renewed link: the unity of faith, the unity of action and mission, the common care for everything that constitutes the task of Church in *statu viae*. A local Church cannot

[40] Much evidence, though analysed from a Roman Catholic point of view, has been gathered by P. Batiffol, *L'Eglise Naissante et le Catholicisme* (Paris 1927)—*La Paix Constantinienne* (Paris 1929)—*Le Siège Apostolique* (Paris 1924)—*Cathedra Petri* (Paris 1938).

[41] It is noteworthy that after having analysed all early Christian evidence on the primacy of Rome, Batiffol reaches an almost identical conclusion—'The papacy of the first centuries is the authority exercised by the Church of Rome among other Churches, authority which consists in caring after their conformity with the authentic tradition of faith . . . and which is claimed by no other church but the Church of Rome'—*Cathedra Petri*, p. 28.

THE PRIMACY OF PETER

isolate herself, become a centre in herself, live 'by herself' and by her own local and private interests, because the *fullness* which constitutes her very being is precisely the fullness of the catholic faith and catholic mission, the fullness of Christ who fills all things in all. The Church cannot realize this fullness, make it her own, and, therefore, be the Church, without *ipso facto* living in all and by all; and this means living in the universal conscience of the Church 'scattered in the whole world and yet abiding as if it were in one home.' A local Church cut from this universal 'koinonia' is indeed a *contradictio in adjecto,* for this koinonia is the very essence of the Church. And it, has, therefore, its *form* and *expression:* primacy. Primacy is the necessary expression of the unity in faith and life of all local Churches, of their living and efficient koinonia.

Now we can return to our first definition of primacy. Primacy *is* power, but as power it is not different from the power of a Bishop in each church. It is not a *higher power* but indeed the same power only expressed, manifested, realized by one. The primate *can* speak for all because the Church is one and because the power he exercises is the power of each bishop and of all bishops. And he *must* speak for all because this very unity and agreement require, in order to be efficient, a special organ of expression, a mouth, a voice. Primacy is thus a necessity because therein is the expression and manifestation of the unity of Churches as being the unity of *the* Church. And it is important to remember that the Primate, as we know him from our canonical tradition, is always the Bishop of a local Church and not a 'bishop at large,' and that primacy belongs to him precisely because of his status in his own Church.[42] It is not a personal charism, but rather a function of the whole Church, carried and fulfilled by its Bishop. The early tradition clearly indicates the primacy of the Church of Rome, yet we know next to nothing about the first Bishops of Rome who, evidently, served as ministers of this primacy. The idea of primacy thus excludes the idea of jurisdictional power but implies that of an 'order' of Churches which does not subordinate one Church to another, but which makes it possible for all Churches to live *together* this life of all in each and of each in all thus by fulfilling the mystery of the Body of Christ, the fullness 'filling all in all.'

[42] cf. G. Florovsky, *The Sacrament of Pentecost,* p. 31.

8

This concept of primacy, as has been said already, is rooted in the 'eucharistic ecclesiology' which we believe to be the source of Orthodox canonical and liturgical tradition. As a result of its distortion or, at least, 'metamorphosis' there appeared another type of ecclesiology which we have termed 'universal.' It leads necessarily to the understanding and practice of primacy as 'supreme power' and, therefore, to a *universal bishop* as source and foundation of jurisdiction in the whole ecclesiastical structure. The Orthodox Church has condemned this distortion in its pure and explicit Roman Catholic form. This does not mean, however, that our church life is free from its poison. The universal ecclesiology is a permanent temptation because in the last analysis it is a *natural* one, being the product of 'naturalization' of Christianity, its adaptation to the life 'after the rudiments of the world, and not after Christ.' Only the historical sources of this temptation in the East are different from those in the West. And inasmuch as all the controversies within Orthodoxy are obviously centred on this basic question of the nature of the Church, we must conclude this article with a short analysis of our own deficiencies.

At a relatively recent date there arose among the Orthodox the opinion that the Church is based in her life on the *principle of autocephaly,* the term 'autocephalous' here being applied exclusively to the Eastern Patriarchates or the great national churches. According to this opinion, the principle of autocephaly is not only one of the historical 'expressions' by the Church of her universal structure, but precisely *the* ecclesiological foundation of the Church and her life. In other words, the unique universal organism of Roman ecclesiology is opposed here to 'autocephalous' organisms, each one constituted by several 'dioceses' under one centre or 'supreme power.' All these 'autocephalies' are absolutely equal among themselves and his equality excludes any universal centre or primacy.[43]

The appearance of this theory and its almost unanimous accept-

[43] The most 'theological' expression of this theory is to be found in the articles, mentioned above, of the Hieromonk Sophrony and E. Kovalevsky. In a more juridical way it is defended by S. V. Troitsky; cf. J. Meyendorff, 'Constantinople and Moscow' in *Tserkovnyi Vestnik,* 16, pp. 5–9. Finally its justification in terms of ecclesiastical nationalism is given by M. Polskii, *The Canonical Status of the Supreme Ecclesiastical Government* (Jordanville, 1948); cf. my essay 'The Church and Ecclesiastical Structure' (Paris 1949).

ance by contemporary Orthodox canonists is very significant. In the first place, the principle of autocephaly has indeed been for the last few centuries the unique principle of organization in Orthodoxy and, therefore, its 'acting' canonical rule. The reason is clear: the 'autocephaly' with this particular meaning is fully adequate to the specifically Eastern form of Christian 'naturalization' or reduction of the Church to the 'natural world.' This explains in turn why of all possible forms it was precisely 'autocephaly' which became for centuries the 'acting canon law' in the Eastern Church and to-day is accepted by so many as an eternal and unchangeable principle of her canonical tradition.

All the deficiencies in the ecclesiology conscience in the East can be ascribed to two major sources: the close 'identification' of the Church with the state (Byzantine 'symphony' and its varieties) and religious nationalism. Both explain the unchallenged triumph of the theory of 'Autocephaly.'

The identification of the Church with the state (cf. the confused and often tragic history of Byzantine theocracy) deeply changed the very notion of *power* in the Church. It was shaped more and more after the 'juridical' pattern of the State, and its understanding as a charismatic ministry within the Body of Christ was consequently weakened. More precisely there occurred a rupture between the sacramental and the jurisdictional power. A bishop, to receive his power, was, of course, still to be consecrated. Yet in fact the source of his 'jurisdictional power' rested now with a 'supreme power' before which he was to become 'responsible.' The bishop's 'report' to the Synod offers the best example of this change as it indicates first the quick transformation of the function of Synod in Byzantium, and second the equally rapid growth of a real 'mystique' of the Supreme Power in the Person of the Patriarch.

We know that in the early Church the synod was by its very nature a gathering of bishops (i.e. a more or less regular convention and not a permanent institution). There were regular or extraordinary synods, but in all of them the essential condition of their very 'function' was the living identity of each bishop and his Church—for it was only as 'head' of his Church, its 'proistamenos' in the deepest sense of this word, that he took part in the synod which thus became the *expression* of the unity and unanimity of the Churches as the Churches of God. Beginning with the fourth century, although not everywhere at the same time, this idea of the synod was progressively replaced by another one: as the supreme and central power *over* the Churches. The best example here is the famous 'synodos endemousa' in Constantinople which became the pattern for the future 'synod.' Brought into existence at first as a synod 'ad hoc'—an occasional meeting of bishops who happenend to be in Constantinople—this synod became little by little a permanent organ of power assisting the Patriarch [44] with the result that the condition for participation in it was reversed: a bishop left his church in order to become a member of this governing body. The bishops became, so to speak, 'power in themselves' and their Synod became the supreme or central power. One step more, and the bishops from the jurisdictional point of view have become representatives or delegates of this high power even in their own Churches. This is, of course, only a scheme, but it would not be difficult to substantiate it with facts.[45] The road from the 'synodos endemousa' to the 'Governing Synod' of the Russian Church is a straight one, complicated, it is true, by influences of the Western and Protestant 'synodal' law. . . . Yet the source of both is in the State, in its notion of 'supreme power' as source of any 'local power.'

Not less characteristic is the development of what may be termed 'patriarchal mystique' which finds its first expression in the development of the power of the Patriarch of Constantinople. In its essence this mystique is radically different from that of Papism. The latter has its roots in the experience of the Church as a universal organism, called to dominate the world; the former in the parallelism of the Church and Empire which required an ecclesiastical 'counterpart' of the Basileus. Although one must stress again and again, that the origin of the Byzantine Patriarch's unique power is not 'lust of power' but the 'byzantine analogy' between the two supreme powers,[46] yet here also it is the State and not the Church that shapes this new idea of power.

---

[44] M. Skaballanovich, *The Byzantine State and the Church in XI Century* (St. Petersburg, 1884, in Russian); E. Gerland, 'Die Vorgeschichte des Patriarchats des Kpl.' in *Byz. Neues Jahrb.*, IX, 218.

[45] I. Sokolov, 'The Election of Bishops in Byzantium' in *Vizantiiskii Vremennik*, 22, 1915–16 (in Russian).

[46] cf. my essays, 'The Destiny of Byzantine Theocracy' in *Pravoslavnaia Mysl'* 6, (in Russian) and 'Byzantine Theocracy and the Orthodox Church,' in *St. Vladimir's Seminary Quarterly*, 1953.

The metamorphosis of the very concept of 'power,' its discon-
nection, even if a partial one, from the ecclesiology of the Body of
Christ and, as the natural result, the emergence of a 'supreme
power'—all this constitutes the first and yet most tragic crisis in
the history of Orthodox ecclesiology. The time has come it seems
to us to admit openly that the Byzantine period of our history,
which in many respects is still for us the golden age of Orthodoxy,
saw, nevertheless, the beginning of an ecclesiological disease. The
mystique of the 'symphonia' (with its only alternative being the
monastic 'desert' and the individual work for 'salvation') obscured
the reality of the Church as People of God, as the Church of God
and the Body of Christ manifested and edified in every place. It
was the triumph of universal ecclesiology in the Byzantine form.

The state and its idea of power are, however, but the first of
the two major causes of that disease. The second, not less important in its consequences, was the growth of *religious nationalism*.
No one, I think, will deny that one of the fruits of Byzantine
Theocracy, which for a long time obscured the life of the Orthodox
East, was the growth of those religious nationalisms which little by
little identified the Church, her structure and organization with the
nation, making her the religious expression of national existence.
This national existence, however natural and therefore legitimate
it may be, is by its very essence a 'partial' existence—the existence
as a 'part' of humanity which though not necessarily inimical to
its other 'parts' is none-the-less opposed to them as 'one's own' to
the 'alien.' The Early Church knew herself to be the *tertium genus*
in which there is neither Greek nor Jew. This means that it proclaimed and conveyed a Life which without rejecting the 'partial'
and natural life could transform it into 'wholeness' or *catholicity.*
Hence it must be clear that religious nationalism is essentially a
heresy about the Church, for it reduces grace and the new life to
'nature' and makes the latter a formal principle of the Church's
structure. This does not mean that there can be no Christian people
or a Christian vocation of a nation; it means only that a Christian
nation (i.e. a nation which has acknowledged its Christian vocation)
does not *become* the Church. Because the nature of the Church is
the Body of Christ, she belongs to the Kingdom of the age to come
and cannot identify herself with anything in 'this world. . . .'

Yet it is precisely this religious nationalism in combination with the new 'statelike' concept of power which supplied the basis for the new theory of autocephaly and made it for centuries the 'acting canon law' in the Orthodox East. Elsewhere I have tried to show the weak points in contemporary attempts to justify this theory and to erect it into an ecclesiological absolute. From the point of view which interests us here, however, the negative significance of this theory (defended, on the one hand, as a justification of the national divisions of Orthodoxy and, on the other, as sanction for the prevalent administrative centralism) introduces into the Orthodox doctrine of the Church the very elements of 'universal ecclesiology' which she rejects and condemns as it is. It obscures the sacramental structure of the Church rooted in its life as Body of Christ, by a 'national' structure, thus making a natural organism.

On the essential falsehood of this theory and on its fateful consequences in the life of the Church much has been written. One can affirm that the ecclesiastical consciousness has never 'received' it as Tradition—as witness about the nature of the Church. Neither the doctrine of the 'five senses' which was the first reaction of Byzantine canonists to Roman claims, nor the absolute 'autocephalism' of national theocraties born as it was out of the fight against the theocracy of Byzantium, nor the synodal regime of the Russian Church—none of these succeeded in being accepted as an organic expression of Church consciousness or in obscuring to the end the genuine and living sources of ecclesiastical life. This source is still in the true canonical tradition and in the sacraments by which the Church lives and realizes herself. . . .

Is it necessary to mention all the harm done to the Church by this acting 'canon law,' disconnected as it is from the living sources of Orthodox ecclesiology? Such as, on the one hand, the bureaucratic spirit pervading the Church, making her the 'religious department'; the absence of a living 'sobornost'; the transformation of dioceses into mere administrative units living under the control of abstract 'centres'; the abyss between the 'power' and the body of the Church and, as the result of this, the 'revolt of the masses'; the introduction into the Church of the ideas of 'representation of the interests' of this or that category be it of the 'lay control' or of the division between clergy and laity, etc. . . . Or on the other hand, the deep and tragic division of Orthodoxy into national Churches each indifferent to the other, living in and by themselves, the crisis of the universal consciousness, and the weakening of the catholic links. . . .

We must hope, however, that this crisis is not a mortal one. The strength of Christ is fulfilled in weakness and the gates of hell cannot prevail against the Church. In sufferings and sorrows there appears to-day a new thirst for the *truth* about the Church, a new interest in discovering the genuine sources of her life. The question which we raised and attempted to answer, however partially and schematically, in this article, that of 'primacy,' cannot be separated from a deep and consistent return to Orthodox ecclesiology.

NICOLAS AFANASSIEFF

THE CHURCH WHICH PRESIDES IN LOVE

I

ORTHODOX Church polemics against the primacy of Rome depend, broadly speaking, on Roman Catholic theology.[1] This is not surprising, since the actual aim of Orthodox theology is to refute arguments put out in favour of Roman primacy. Now the Catholic doctrine of primacy is founded on their doctrine of the primacy of the Apostle Peter: and therefore Orthodox theologians concentrate their attention on this subject. Exegesis of New Testament texts on the position of Peter results in a discussion between Orthodox and Catholic theologians. Meanwhile, a similar discussion has arisen concerning the oldest Patristic evidence about the Church of Rome. Rome's role in history is also under dispute, and so far no agreement has been reached on the matter. No one denies, to-day, that she has held a leading position, but we have still to ask what position it was and what was its nature. In other words, we started discussing the primacy of Rome before we raised the question: what is primacy itself? Can primacy—whether of Rome or any other church—really exist in the Church? Here is the really important question, and the answer, whether positive or negative, will help us to work out our own views of the Church of Rome. If we are to solve the problem of primacy within the Church, our starting-point must be from ecclesiology; i.e. we must ask, does the doctrine of the Church contain the idea of primacy (in present or any other form), or exclude it altogether? This method can be used to solve problems of exegesis and of history too; it is really the most natural approach, for the problem of primacy is inherent in the doctrine of the Church. We can thus pose the problem of primacy in general, for Orthodox and Catholics alike. But we must not think of such a method as involving any renunciation (even provisional) of our confessional allegiances. That sort of thing

[1] In this essay I develop ideas which I have already published in an article 'La doctrine de la primauté à la lumière de l'ecclesiologie' in *Istina* 1957, No. 4. Some passages are literally transcribed.

57

would only be possible for a bad Orthodox or a bad Catholic. As we study the problem of primacy in general, and especially the primacy of Rome, we must not be ruled by polemical motives: the problem is to be solved to satisfy ourselves and Orthodox theology. The solution of the problem is urgent, since Orthodox theology has not yet built up any systematic doctrine on Church government. And although we have a doctrine concerning Ecumenical Councils regarded as organs of government in the Church, we shall see presently that our doctrine is not enough to refute the Catholic doctrine of primacy.

2

1. Approaching our solution of the problem of primacy by a method which we might call 'ecclesiological,' we are at once faced with a great difficulty: several systems of ecclesiology have grown up in the course of history. And the Church, although itself the subject of all these systems, is understood by each of them in a different way. Therefore, inevitably, the problem of primacy must be differently stated and resolved in each system—and then the several systems often will turn out to be just different facets of the same ecclesiological theory.

The systems can all be reduced to two fundamental types: universal ecclesiology and eucharistic ecclesiology. The universal sort is now predominant, especially in Catholic doctrine. The Orthodox Church has not clearly defined her attitudes, but our 'school' teaching follows Catholic doctrine and accepts universal ecclesiology as an axiom.

According to universal ecclesiology, the Church is a single organic whole, including in itself all church-units of any kind, especially those headed by bishops. This organic whole is the Body of Christ or, to return to Catholic theological terms, the Mystical Body of Christ. Such a concept of the Church has become a habit of thought and we never question it; we are more inclined to use it to furnish premises on which to build all theological discussions about the Church. But as for finding out the relationship between the different church units, particularly the diocesan church and the universal Church—*that* question is still not quite clarified. Usually the church units are regarded as parts of the universal Church: less usually people see in each church a *pars pro toto*, or again a detached fragment, *ein Splitter*.[2] In the Russian ecclesiological system of our time, the episcopal church (the diocese) forms one part of the autocephalous Russian Church. The Moscow Council of 1917–18 decided that 'the diocese is defined as one part of the Russian Orthodox Church, when governed by a bishop according to canon law.'

Their definition of the diocese alone is incontestable proof that the members of the Council were taking their stand on universal ideology, and that they went further in this respect than people at Byzantium. According to the prevalent Byzantine point of view, patriarchates were made up of a number of metropolitan units, and a metropolis was made up of diocesan churches. As history went on, the metropolis tended to decay and the power of the patriarchs increased, but the diocesan churches were always regarded as fundamental units which made up a patriarchate. Hence at Byzantium it was unthinkable for any one to define the diocese (officially at least) as they did at Moscow. When Byzantium was already in decline, a theory arose of the κηδεμονία πάντων. The whole of the Orthodox Church was to be one organic unit with the Patriarch of Constantinople at its head. The bishops, especially metropolitan bishops, were to be no more than his delegates. The proposed doctrine was out of step with the march of history and did not influence Church order.

2. The basic principles of the 'world-wide' theory of the Church were formulated by Cyprian of Carthage. A Roman by education and habit, Cyprian may have thought that the mere empirical unity of a number of local churches could not be properly guaranteed. The numbers had increased so much, compared with what they were in the time of the Apostles, that Tertullian could now tell the Roman world (with a touch of exaggeration, of course), 'The Christian newcomers have filled the place up: cities, islands, fortresses, boroughs, camp and Senate-house, palace and forum— leaving the pagans nothing but their temples.' The 'Ecumenical Church' (i.e. a number of local churches united by concord and love), though a generally accepted idea in Cyprian's time, must have been too vague for him, with his Roman training in precise legal

[2] See O. Linten, *Das Problem der Urkirche in der neuer Forschung,* Uppsala, 1932; F. M. Braun, *Aspects nouveaux du problème de l'Eglise,* Fribourg, 1942 (translation from the German *Neues Licht auf die Kirche,* 1946).

formulae. He saw that the concord of local churches was often broken in daily fact; concord turned into discord, and love into enmity. Human vanity and ambition were leading heretics and schismatics far away from the church, tearing and weakening it in the process. On the other hand there seemed another possibility, in Cyprian's eyes, a different unity which seemed next to perfect. Cyprian did not have to live through the awful drama forced on Jerome and his contemporaries, who really came to believe that the fall of Rome would mean the fall of the whole civilized world. Rome was still there, solidly established: the portents foreboding crisis could not yet be observed by the men of Cyprian's time. The entire οἰκουμένη—the inhabited earth, the then universe, was transformed and made one single entity by the strength of the Roman Imperial idea: they were one Roman Empire. The government of Rome had gradually become a world-wide system: the whole world looked to her for its fate. Different parts would be able to live their own lives and even enjoy some autonomy, but they could not break up the organic singleness of the Empire; imperially considered, they were secondary elements. The Roman Empire formed the σῶμα, and the Emperor was its soul. The concept of the Empire was Cyprian's inspiration, though he may not have known it, and the foundation for his doctrine of Church unity. We moderns can no longer imagine the enormous fascination of the Imperial Idea, as leading Church figures felt it then. Cyprian turned over a new page of history by his doctrine of Church unity, but he also stood on the border-line between two periods: besides having a natural attachment to his own age and to all the Church's past, he was fired by new thoughts when it came to his doctrine of the Church.

To Cyprian, as to Ignatius and Tertullian, the Church is one because Christ is one: *Deus unus est et Christus unus, et una ecclesia.*[3] Here was truth unquestionable, and neither Cyprian nor his contemporaries doubted it. Cyprian was a bishop first and foremost, trying to apply the doctrine of Church unity to the changes and chances of the day. He was less interested in the theoretical aspects or intrinsic value of the doctrine. The Church in its empiric *esse*, the one and only Church, appeared to exist in the form of a multitude of churches. How could the unity of the Church be pre-

---

[3] Epist. XLIII, V, 2; cf. Tertullian, *De Virg.*, 2.

served despite the multiplicity of churches? Cyprian answered the question by applying St. Paul's doctrine to these many churches, i.e. the doctrine of the organic nature of the Church's body. Just as we can distinguish members in the Church, the Body of Christ, so the one and only Church, physically speaking, is made up of different local churches, which are her limbs or members: *ecclesia per totum mundum in multa membra divisa.*[4] The Church is naturally ecumenical, since it spreads all over the world and embraces all the churches—those flourishing at a given time, and churches of the past and future as well. Fullness and unity are the possessions of this Church scattered *per totum mundum;* not of isolated local churches which, being merely *members* of the Church, can only possess part of that fullness. Any local church is not the 'Catholic' Church, as Ignatius of Antioch taught: the local churches taken all together form the universal ecumenical Church, i.e. the Catholic Church. So the sense of the term 'Catholic Church' has changed; or, more accurately, the concept of 'Church' has changed, while the concept καθολικός is the same as it was for Ignatius. For this reason 'Catholic Church,' empirically speaking, means the same thing to Cyprian as 'Ecumenical Church'—the Church on earth at a given time. All the local churches together are the one and only Body of Christ, but the empirical Church is to some extent the sum of its separate parts. Hence Cyprian could speak of *conexa et ubique coniuncta unitas catholicae ecclesiae,*[5] the unity of the Catholic Church, tied together and cohering. The different parts or members of this Church are joined (conexa) like the branches of a single tree or put together (conjuncta) like the simple words in a compound word. Cyprian also describes all the local churches taken together as the composite unity of the Church's body, *compago corporis ecclesiastici;*[6] a union, or whole, comparable to the union of a human soul and body. We might say that the empirical whole, the *compositum* (*compago*), is the body of the Catholic Church.

The universal Church, therefore, having catholicity as one of its attributes, is a single being divided into various parts. While remaining one, this being manifests itself in everyday life as an

[4] Epist. LV, XXIV, 2; cf. Epist. XXXVI, IV, 1. Omnes enim nos decet pro corpore totius ecclesiae cuius per varias quasque provincias membra digesta sunt, excubare.
[5] Epist. LV, XXIV, 2.
[6] Epist. LV, XXIV, 3.

assembly of local churches, but its unity is maintained. Cyprian was concerned to know how and why: his quest for an answer led him to construct his theory of the universal Church. Cyprian found his answer in a doctrine of episcopal unity built on almost the same lines as the doctrine of Church unity. The Church is one because there is one God, one Christ, one faith. *Episcopatus unus est*[7] because 'the throne of Peter is one,'[8] 'in which God has established and shown the source of all unity.'[9] 'There is one God alone, one Christ, one Church, one Throne of Peter, whom the word of the Lord had made his foundation-stone.'[10] This Throne of Peter is held by the whole episcopate, so that every bishop is Peter's successor, but only in so far as he is part of the episcopate. Cyprian uses the lawyer's term *in solidum* when he affirms *Episcopatus unus est, cuius a singulis in solidum pars tenetur*:[11] that is, every member of the one episcopate possesses the chair of Peter in common with his fellows. In actual life the episcopate is made manifest in a multiplicity of bishops. 'Just as the one Church of Christ is divided into many members over all the world, so the one episcopate is expanded into a multiplicity of many bishops united in concord.'[12] Perhaps it would be more exact to re-state Cyprian's thought like this: the division of the Catholic Church into local churches is the practical result of diffusing the one episcopate into a visible multiplicity of bishops. Every bishop presides separately over his own local church, but all bishops have possession of Peter's throne together and so form a 'multiplicity in concord' (*concors numerositas*). The sum of the local churches form a *corpus* in which each church is joined to all the rest by very strong ties: in the same way the bishops too form a *corpus* in which each bishop is joined to all the rest by the harmony prevailing throughout the entire episcopate. Full and perfect concord, a

[7] De Unit. V.
[8] Epist. XLIII, V, 2.
[9] Epist. XLIII, VII, 1.
[10] Epist. XLIII, V, 2.
[11] De Unit. V.
[12] Epist. LV, XXIV, 2: 'et cum sit a Christo una ecclesia per totum mundum in multa membra divisa, item epispocatus unus episcoporum multorum concordi numerositate *diffusus*. . . .' My own text gives a literal translation. I quote the more polished version of Canon Bayard: 'Seeing therefore that by Christ's institution there is one Church only in all the world, spread abroad in many members, and one episcopate only, represented by a multiplicity of bishops one in fellowship together . . .' (St. Cyprien, *Correspondence*, II, Paris, 1925, p. 147).

quasi-musical harmony, is, in historical fact, to bind the bishops in one.[13] In an ideal world, the unity of the episcopate derives from the unity of the Church: in actual fact the unity of the episcopate preserves the unity of local churches, since concord among the bishops ties, or rather welds all these churches into mutual fellowship. Union of the bishops in concord produces a single entirety: and the 'symphonic multiplicity' of the bishops in turn makes the local churches into a single entirety. No wonder Cyprian attached such exceptional importance to concord! In his eyes there was no possibility of discord between bishops, because of their common possession of Peter's throne: in effect, this common possession really implies the summary banishment of a member no longer in accord with the rest, and therefore no longer qualified for his share in the episcopate. In this manner, concord and unity are for ever unbroken.

The Church of Cyprian's doctrine might well be compared to a truncated cone: the large inferior base of the cone would be the numerous but united local churches, and the small top platform the 'multiplicity united in concord' of the bishops. Every point on the large base where there is a local church, a member of the universal Church, has its corresponding point on the smaller and higher plane in the bishop, a member of the episcopate: put the other way round, each part of the episcopate (bishop) is responsible for one part of the universal Church. The unity of the top and bottom planes is maintained by their ties with one another. Each may become larger or smaller, but always related to the other, so that if the top level increases in size the bottom does too, and *vice versa*. If any point or part of either level became detached, there would be a corresponding fraction in the other: the cone would then be reduced in size, though still a cone, but the broken-off section would then be outside the cone.

Cyprian defines the relation between bishop and church in a famous phrase: 'It must be known that the bishop is in the Church and the Church in the bishop: any person who is not with the bishop is not in the Church.' [14] A bishop cannot exist without a Church, but also a Church cannot exist cut off from its bishop: the

[13] Epist. LIX, XIV, 2: concordia cohaerens.
[14] Epist. LXVI, VIII, 3: Scire debes episcopum in ecclesia esse et ecclesiam in episcopo et si qui cum episcopo non sit in ecclesia non esse.

bottom side of the cone cannot be detached from its top. The top cannot exist by itself, for then the throne of Peter would have no Church in which to be. No more can the base exist without its top, for then the Church would be living without Peter's throne, which Christ founded to hold its unique position there. The Universal Church is the entire truncated cone, and not just one of its surfaces.

There is plenty of logic in Cyprian's doctrine, but logic by itself is no proof of the truth. So arguments in favour of Cyprian's system must not be founded only on its logical character—its more-or-less logical character, rather assuming that Cyprian's system has been left logically incomplete. In this, however, Cyprian shows the greatest of his doctrinal virtues; an intimate awareness of the Church was the root of his own life; he could not let go the traditional doctrine of the Church to round off his system. He did not draw from that system the conclusions it implied; any more than he did in general for the other doctrines he put forward. Cyprian's genius comes out in his active Church life more than it does in his theological thought. To posterity he has left an ideal picture of 'the Bishop' which shines so bright and clear that our minds really see it; he has left us a literary heritage broken by frequent self-contradiction, which has been a matter for controversy from then till the present day. The truncated cone is incomplete in itself. Cyprian had all the *data* for making his cone perfect: according to his doctrine there should have really been one single bishop at the head of the Universal Church. He was unwilling to place the Bishop of Rome outside the *concors numerositas* of bishops and yet the place given by him to the Roman Church did raise it above the 'harmonious multitude.' The ideal 'Peter's throne' occupied by the whole episcopate became confused in Cyprian's mind with the actual throne occupied by the Bishop of Rome. According to Cyprian, every bishop occupies Peter's throne (the Bishop of Rome among others) but the See of Rome is Peter's throne *par excellence.* The Bishop of Rome is the direct heir of Peter, whereas the others are heirs only indirectly, and sometimes only by the mediation of Rome. Hence Cyprian's insistence that the Church of Rome is the root and matrix of the Catholic Church.[15] The subject is treated in so many of Cyprian's passages that there is no doubt: to him, the See of Rome was *ecclesia principalis unde unitas sacerdotalis exorta*

[15] Epist. XLVIII, III, 1 : Ecclesiae catholicae matricem et radicem.

est.[16] But he does not proceed to draw any clear conclusions from his doctrine about the See of Rome. Being so keenly aware of the Church's factual life, Cyprian could not deny that the See of Rome held a preponderant position : but he was intuitively in step with trends in the whole Church which did not allow him to make the Bishop of Rome head of the episcopate. The Bishop of Rome undertook to relieve him, and draw the necessary conclusions himself. Logically it was inevitable. If the Universal Church as Cyprian saw it can be compared to a truncated cone, we must admit that the upper plane is in fact above the multitude of local churches. It is at the head of the multitude, so to speak, because the power in the Church belongs to it and, through it, also belongs to each bishop in his church. The world-wide unity of the Church cannot be built up on the model of the Roman imperial unity unless we bring in the fundamental principle which held the Empire together —lawful right. Cyprian certainly brought a legal element into his consideration of power inside the Church, but he refused to stretch it to cover the relationship of bishops with one another. The *concors numerositas* of bishops constitutes the power within the Church, but within its own membership it disallows the power element. The bishops are not subordinated to one another, but mutually united on a foundation of concord. No wonder Cyprian's system turned out a historical failure! In his declining years Cyprian was to see his system crash before his own eyes. He saw that the *concors numerositas* was only an ideal; in real life there is certainly *numerositas,* but not concord, since a *concors numerositas* cannot work without a head.

3. I have dwelt at length on the interpretation of Cyprian's theory of the Church for two reasons. As I said above, he was the first to formulate the principle of a universal theory of the Church. More important still, Cyprian did not succeed in constructing his system without some idea of primacy, and this shows that if a universal theory of the Church is adhered to, the doctrine of primacy will somehow be a necessary concomitant. A single body must be crowned by a single head, showing in his own person the unity of the whole system. If we take the universal theory of the Church, we cannot refute the doctrine of universal primacy just by saying that the Church has Christ as Head; that is

[16] Epist. LIX, XIV, 1.

E

an indisputable truth, and supporters of primacy do not themselves oppose it. The real question is: If the Church has an invisible Head (Christ) can she, or can she not, also have a visible head? If not, then why can a local church have a single head in the person of its bishop? In other words, why can one part of the Universal Church have a single head, while the entire Universal Church is deprived of one? This question should be specially relevant in discussing autocephalous Orthodox churches and their problems. If there is no primacy in the Universal Church, why do we allow a partial primacy within the boundaries of an auto-cephalous church? The head of an autocephalous church makes manifest its unity: but how can the unity of the whole Orthodox Church be given empiric expression in the absence of a universal primacy? Orthodox theology makes it a point of principle that the Universal Church should be directed by Ecumenical Councils. Obviously, Orthodox theology has made Cyprian's doctrine her own (in part at least): for he constructed the only theological foundations upon which a theory of councils in the Church could rest. Even so, his doctrine on Councils remains as incomplete as the rest of his system. The *concors numerositas* of the bishops is naturally manifested in the councils, where their concord should find means of expression. But the concord is only an ideal one, if the element of jurisdiction is never present in the relations between bishops. Also, the decisions of the Council have no real weight if they are not founded on legal right. How can they ever be put in force, and by whom? Cyprian certainly thought that these decisions were put into practice by the bishops, who were members of the Council and invested with power inside the local churches. The thing was possible, provided the power of the bishops had rested upon a juridical basis, but in Cyprian's time no such basis yet existed: or only in his mind, not in real life. What is even more important, if Councils are to manifest the unity of the episcopate, they presuppose primacy within the episcopal body. Without it, who would convoke the councils? Cyprian never asked himself that question, just as he never remarked on his own actual posses-sion of the primacy in North Africa, though that primacy was much more worthy of the name than the primacy of the Bishop of Rome over Italian affairs. We should note that the councils have not been the same in the course of centuries: they have undergone great

changes. Cyprian started a new form of councils, episcopal con-
ferences; but his own mental picture saw them in the shape of a
diocesan synod enriched by the presence of other bishops. For this
reason he was able to avoid asking a whole row of further questions, like how was the council to be convoked and in what way
could its decisions be practically applied. Cyprian's Doctrine of
Councils was to be completed by others and its final shape was
something he could never have foreseen: the Church of the
Empire worked it out, and the council of bishops became the
council of the Empire.

The conciliar idea cannot be set up against primacy: a council
does not merely not exclude primacy, it actually presupposes it.
The councils cannot be gathered together automatically; they must
be convoked by the head of the diocese.[17] If there had been no
single heads in the autocephalous churches, councils could never
have existed; otherwise, anarchy would have reigned, with every
bishop thinking he had a right to convoke councils. The Ecumenical
Councils were not 'at the head' of the Church; even in the period
of their greatest importance, they did not regard themselves as
organs for directing the Church. An ecumenical council was certainly the highest institution in the Church: it tackled dogmatic
problems and determined the basic principles of ecclesiastical order
and discipline. Still, if they were to stand really at the head of the
Church the ecumenical councils should have been permanent, and
not convoked in such a random way. The setting up of a council
(whether diocesan or ecumenical) assumes that some permanent
head of the Church is there already. It is now commonly accepted
that the right of convoking councils belonged to the emperor. However considerable in numbers, a council was still not considered to
be a real ecumenical council unless the Emperor had convoked it.
The letters of Pope Leo the Great and the emperors Theodosius
and Marcian are of great interest here: the Pope, in spite of not
recognizing the Council of Ephesus in 449, dared not convoke an
ecumenical council himself; all he did was to make insistent state-
ments to the emperors that such a convocation was necessary. The
Emperor Marcian, after his accession, decided to convoke a council;
and Pope Leo had to bow to the Emperor's opinion, although he
thought a convocation would be ill-timed just then, when there had

[17] See the Nineteenth Canon of the Council of Antioch.

been so many changes both in Church and State. No matter how we define the place of the Roman or Byzantine emperor in the Church, we must accept the fact that he really was, in some ways, the head of the Church-in-the-Empire. Of course it was not primacy that the Emperor held claim to; primacy is an exclusively Church affair and can only belong to a bishop. But if the ecumenical church (the church dwelling inside the boundaries of the Empire) had not had the emperor at its head, ecumenical councils would not have taken place in fact or in principle. When the force of events had turned the ecumenical council into a purely Church institution, councils could not be convoked except where primacy in fact already existed: thus in the West, councils continued to exist even after the separation of the churches, because the primacy of the Bishop of Rome was firmly established there. In the East there were no more ecumenical councils. All attempts to convoke a Pan-Orthodox council in our own age have ended in obstructions, and it is rather unlikely that such a council could ever be convoked. This is due to the absence of a primacy capable of commanding recognition by all the Orthodox churches. There is no Pan-Orthodox Head of the Church, consequently any convocation of a council is a practical impossibility. Supposing that the leaders of the autocephalous churches should all agree to allow a patriarch to convoke an ecumenical council, their action would imply that this patriarch was recognized as primate of the Orthodox Church. I shall put off any attempt to decide whether the Patriarch of Constantinople has the right to convoke a council, and confine myself to a single remark: ever since the ninth century the *de facto* position of the Patriarch of Constantinople has favoured his claim to this right, and yet the Patriarch is well known never to have convoked an ecumenical council: he has never even explored the possibilities of planning such a convocation. One thing is clear: if the auto-cephalous churches had recognized the right of the Patriarch of Constantinople to convoke, they would simultaneously have recognized his primacy in the Orthodox Church.

I must once more point out the incorrectness of basing arguments against primacy on the conciliar principle. Orthodox theologians are none-the-less right in emphasizing the principle, because it defines both the nature and the limitations of primacy. The conciliar principle serves to limit the power of the primate-bishop, but we must not think this is a hard and fast limitation in legal terms. There is another way to describe it. The bishop possessing primacy acts with the agreement of the whole body of bishops : this agreement is made manifest in the council in which the primate bishop participates as its president. In Orthodox theology the patriarch is conceived as being *primus inter pares* among the bishops. This formula, though generally allowed, is misleading, and it would be difficult to find justification for it anywhere in the history of the Orthodox Church. It is indeed doubtful that the bishops ever thought themselves the equals of the patriarch in every respect, or that he thought himself their equal. Equality is really a difficult claim, when the patriarch possesses rights of which the other bishops are deprived. A fairer statement (to use language borrowed from Cyprian of Carthage) would be : the patriarch as member of the episcopate of the autocephalous church is not above it, but as its leader he is first in the episcopal body.

4. The decline of the conciliar principle led to another type of universal doctrine of the Church : we might call it 'pontifical.' In the West traces of this doctrine can be found quite early. It becomes dominant after the Council of Trent, which confirmed the idea that the Bishop of Rome had sovereignty over the council. The Pope is superior to the council : the conciliar principle is therefore wiped out. The councils, if they occur, are no longer councils in the true sense of the word, and become advisory agencies supporting the Bishop of Rome. The accord of the episcopate remains a matter of importance, but the Pope is not juridically bound by the decisions of his council. The Pope, being placed above the council, becomes superior to all the other bishops and turns into a 'super-bishop.' But the doctrine concerning bishops is founded on divine law (those are the terms used in Catholic canon law) and still retains its full validity. At the present day we are witnessing various attempts to introduce important changes into the universal doctrine of the Church, and these changes would affect one particular sphere—the doctrine of episcopacy. According to Catholic and Orthodox theology, a bishop holds first place in the ecclesiastical hierarchy. To him belongs the highest sacerdotal degree; the second degree belongs to the priesthood. Whatever the powers of the bishop may be in matters of government, in matters of liturgy the sum of his powers is always constant. On this principle the powers

of patriarchs, autocephalous church leaders, and even popes are identical, liturgically speaking, with the powers of all other bishops. Theologians of to-day always agree that the difference between a bishop and a priest, in the sphere of liturgy, has one essential or even exclusive characteristic: that is, the priest cannot celebrate the Sacrament of Ordination. Consequently certain well-defined powers in matters of liturgy are attached to both classes, and these powers must remain unchanged.

Some thirty years ago documents were found proving that in the fifteenth century the popes used to allow the abbots of certain abbeys a right to ordain not only minor clerics, but priests as well, in order to serve the needs of their abbeys. This discovery was a sensation in Catholic circles and caused some embarrassment. Clearly the discovery was to be extremely important to Catholic dogma: it saps the very foundations of the doctrine which declares that bishops alone are entitled to conduct ordinations of priests. We now know that the superiors of certain abbeys (in other words, priests and not bishops) were able to ordain other priests. The deduction follows: the reason why priests have no right to ordain other priests is not a dogmatic reason but more a question of discipline. The *sacerdotium* with which the priests were invested at their ordination did confer power on them to celebrate the Sacrament of Ordination, but the ecclesiastical authorities debarred them from making use of this spiritual capacity, and the bar was a disciplinary one. If we acknowledge that priests have at least a theoretical right to conduct ordinations, should we not admit that there is no difference between priests and bishops where liturgy is concerned, i.e. we have only one degree of *sacerdotium* before us, not two? In that case, the bishop will be nothing but a priest who has been given wider powers in the sphere of jurisdiction.

What are the possible results of such a doctrine of priests and bishops? A contemporary Catholic theologian writes: 'Christians must be more than ever one, they must more than ever take their stand in face of all the problems of life, there must be more unanimity in action than ever: one man alone can direct, one alone can teach, one alone command—Peter and his successors. We must not be surprised at this: the former responsibility of the bishop in his diocese is gradually changing hands; and to-day the Pope will take it over as his own mission; it would not be good, either for the

Church or the world, if different, sometimes even conflicting, ideas were adopted by each different diocese. If the Church wants to remain one in a world in process of unification, then the Papacy must speak often and guide all. For this reason, the twentieth century is a new dawn in the Church, the dawn of a new age, a Pontifical age, as it is also the dawn of a comprehensive world and an international society: just as separate states will disappear, so bishops will lose their sovereignty, and leave to Peter and his successors the general guidance of the whole Catholic movement and their whole apostolic charge.' [18] We are indeed witnessing the birth of a new age in the Catholic Church—the birth of a universo-pontifical ecclesiology. This new type of ecclesiology is the normal development of universal ecclesiology to its absolute form: on the other hand, it can be interpreted as a sort of return to the traditional ecclesiology, though the tradition has undergone much change and some distortion. The great primitive ecclesiastical maxim was that in the Church there must be one bishop only. Ignatius of Antioch gave special importance to the formula 'One God, one Christ, one faith, one altar, and one bishop.' We shall presently see that Ignatius, in writing these words, had in mind the local church, and that his ecclesiological context was not at all the same as the Universal ecclesiology. If the Universal Church is a sole body and if we accept Ignatius's statement, we cannot avoid coming to the conclusion that in the Universal Church there must be one single bishop, and that according to Catholic doctrine he can be no other than the Bishop of Rome. In the capacity of being bishop of all the Universal Church, he takes the place of all the other bishops. In consequence, the others become mere administrative instruments, used by the Pope for governing the innumerable parishes led by presbyters.

It is still too soon to tell if Rome is likely to sponsor this new ecclesiology, which is sturdily opposed to Catholic theological circles.[19] What matters to me is simply the fact that this trend

[18] J. Beyer, S.J., 'Le souverain Pontife, centre vital et unité de l'Eglise,' *Textes des conférences données au congrès eucharistique des dirigeants de la Croisade eucharistique en août 1955 à Nivelles* Monthly bulletin of the Directors of the C.E. 24, 1955, n. 2, p. 38. I quote after B. Luykx, O. Praem, 'De l'évêque' in *Questions Liturgiques et paroissiales*, 4–5, 1956.

[19] See Dom O. Rousseau 'La vraie valeur de l'épiscopat dans l'Eglise,' and Dom B. Botte 'Presbyterium' et 'Ordo episcoporum' in *Irenikon* I, XXIX, 1956.

exists in ecclesiological theory. I cannot discuss these new trends here, they would take me too far from the main point. This type of ecclesiology must start with the doctrine of bishops, which is quite a different subject. Furthermore the ecclesiology of a Universal Pontiff no longer contains any real doctrine of primacy, whatever meaning we attach to the word; for primacy presupposes a multiplicity of bishops among whose number one holds the primacy.

5. We can now form our first conclusions. Universal ecclesiology (which says that the entire Church on earth is a unique living body) contains in itself the doctrine of a single man as head of the Church. It must be admitted that the doctrine of Primacy is quite incontestable if you start from Universal ecclesiology. But even so, we can maintain a controversy with the Catholic Church, of the very highest importance; but only because primacy in the Church, according to Catholic theology, has no actual being unless it means the primacy of Rome. If there had been no Roman primacy, no other primacy could have existed; that is the Catholic view. Even granting that in fact the primacy did belong to Rome, such an admission of mere *fact* would not have been nearly enough for Catholic theologians: they might indeed have thought it more dangerous than a plain denial. Catholic theology requires us to admit the *dogmatic* assertion which says that primacy in the Church solely belongs to the See of Rome. But from another view, to deny the primacy of the Bishop of Rome does not necessarily involve denying the very idea of primacy. Far from it; so long as we stay in the sphere of universal ecclesiology, we must admit the idea of primacy in the Universal Church, though we should remember that the terms of stating it may be extremely varied. Oscar Cullmann is most significant on this subject: he resolutely rejects the dogmatic doctrine of the primacy of Rome, but still admits that primacy may exist in the Universal Church.[20] The Orthodox theologian A. W. Kartscheff is of equal significance: he makes an equally categorical denial of the primacy of Rome, but has lately made a most resolute pronouncement in favour of the primacy of Constantinople within the bounds of the Orthodox Church.[21] Both

[20] O. Cullmann, *Saint Pierre, disciple-apôtre-martyr,* Neuchâtel and Paris, 1952, pp. 213–15.

[21] A. W. Kartacheff, 'La réunion de l'Orthodoxie' (in Russian) in *Tserkovnyi Vestnik,* 1956, no. 5–6, pp. 4–12.

affirmations witness that the doctrine of primacy derives, in a logical way, from the universal ecclesiology.

3

1. The influence of universal ecclesiology is so strong that it seems to theologically-minded people the only possible approach: almost an ecclesiological category, without which any thought about the Church seems impossible. If universal ecclesiology is the only conceivable form, it must have been there from the beginning: but this line of argument will lead us to carry back our ecclesiology into a period when it really did not exist, and a whole string of anachronisms will inevitably follow, distorting the perspectives of history. Universal ecclesiology, however, is *not* the only one; what is more, it is not primitive ecclesiology, but quite the reverse: it has taken the place of a different ecclesiology which I call eucharistic.

To begin with I will recall a historical fact: in the apostolic age, and throughout the second and third centuries, every local church was autonomous and independent; autonomous, for it contained in itself everything necessary to its life; and independent by not depending on any other local church or any bishop whatever outside itself. We ought not to regard this autonomy and independence just as a historical fact, due to chance or to the defects of Church organization, then in its infancy—defects that disappeared when the organization took better shape and was more clearly defined. The development did in fact occur; but it does not follow that the organization of the primitive church was defective. In the subsequent history of Church organization there was indeed a change, a change of underlying axiom: in other words, the doctrine of the Church (which gave the axioms of Church organization) suffered change. Of course you can always deny the historical fact itself, or see a myth in it, but only at the price of setting *a priori* concepts above historical realities.

Well, if the autonomy and independence of primitive local churches were not due to chance, how can we account for them? If we begin with a universal ecclesiology, we can do nothing at all: one part of the Church—in this system, a local church—cannot possibly be autonomous or independent, for autonomy and independence are attributes of a whole. Therefore the primitive churches were autonomous and independent in virtue of the fact that each local church was the Church of God in all its fullness. This conception of the nature of the local church implies the existence of an ecclesiological system, from which the concept of the Universal Church (at least in its existing form) is absent. And without this concept, the Universal Church cannot be mentioned at all.

2. We should never have found the idea of the Universal Church in the New Testament, and least of all in St. Paul's writing, if it had not been already present in our minds. I cannot pause here to analyse the New Testament texts referring to the Church, and show that they do not contain the concept of the Universal Church. The task would be elaborate and serve only to start up arguments about the interpretation of this or that text. I think it will be more useful if I confine myself to explaining the main principles of eucharistic ecclesiology, a subject on which I have had frequent occasion to speak.

'Ye are the Body of Christ' (1 Cor. 12: 27). When the Apostle Paul wrote to tell the Corinthians that they were the Body of Christ, he surely cannot have helped thinking of the liturgical formula 'This is my Body,' which he quotes in the same epistle. Scholars even now disagree about the sense in which 'body' ($\sigma\tilde{\omega}\mu\alpha$) should be taken in St. Paul—the Pauline sense is still difficult and open to discussion—but a comparative study of the two formulas gives us the key to St. Paul's ecclesiology. 'This is my Body' was the eucharistic formula received by Paul from the Church at Jerusalem; it had been spoken every time that the 'Lord's Supper' was celebrated. Even if it was not actually *spoken* in the Church of Jerusalem (which is most unlikely) it was certainly in the minds of all who shared in the Supper. When the Eucharist is celebrated the bread becomes the Body of Christ, and by the bread the partakers become the Body of Christ. 'The loaf which we break, is it not a communion in the Body of Christ? Forasmuch as the loaf is one, we are one body, many though we be: for we are all partakers of that one loaf' (1 Cor. 10: 16–17). The close tie between the loaf of bread and the Body of Christ comes out very clearly here. It is hard to see how 'body' in Paul's 'Ye are the body of Christ' (1 Cor. 12: 27) could mean anything different in 1 Cor. 10: 16–17. The local church—though 'many' and 'ye' in the texts quoted above—is the body of Christ in its eucharistic aspect. This conclusion is, to start with, obviously of the highest importance, for its bearing on the doctrine of the Eucharist: the eucharistic bread *is,* here, the real body of Christ. But it is also important with regard to the doctrine of the Church. Every 'local' church is the Church of God in Christ, for Christ dwells in His Body in the congregation at the Eucharist, and the faithful become members of His Body by virtue of communicating in the Body of Christ. The indivisibility of Christ's Body implies the fullness of the Church dwelling in each of the 'local' churches. This view of the Church is expressed in another of Paul's formulas: 'the Church of God which *is* (or dwells) at Corinth,' or anywhere else where local churches are to be found.

To return to a point mentioned before: the local church is autonomous and independent, because the Church of God in Christ indwells it in perfect fullness. It is independent, because any power, of any kind, exercised over it would be exercised over Christ and His Body. It is autonomous, because fullness of being belongs to the Church of God in Christ, and outside it nothing is, for nothing can have being outside Christ.

At first sight, this eucharistic doctrine may look paradoxical, but the paradox does not attach to the Church; it is in our own empirical consciousness. The fact is that a large number of local churches *do* exist, in empirical reality, as they did in the days of the Apostles. Does this mean that *one* Church cannot exist, only a *number* of Churches of God in Christ? the impossibility of such a conclusion is absolutely clear: there cannot be a plurality of Churches of God in Christ, for Christ is one, and unique. We could not very well apply Euclidean arithmetic, since ecclesiology works with quantities that cannot be reckoned up. 'One plus one is two' is something we are used to in empirical consciousness, but where ecclesiology is concerned, to add up the local churches would be a waste of time. We should always have a total no larger than each item of the addition sum. 'One plus one is still *one*' in ecclesiology. Every local church manifests all the fullness of the Church of God, because it *is* the Church of God and not just one part of it. There may be a plurality of such manifestations, but the Church of God itself remains one and unique always, for it always equals itself. Perhaps this is the time for me to repeat what I had occasion to write elsewhere: 'Every local church enjoys all the fullness of the Church of God in Christ. The plurality of local churches does not destroy the unity of the Church of God, just as the plurality of eucharistic assemblies does not destroy the unity of the Eucharist in time and space. In the Church, unity and plurality are not only overcome: the one also contains the other. The unity of the Church in its empirical life is manifested by a plurality of local churches, and the plurality of the local churches safeguards the unity of the Church of God in Christ. If the number of local churches is increased or diminished, the Church's unity and fullness remains unchanged; there will just be a variation in the number of its manifestations in empirical existence. This number of manifestations of the Church makes up its exterior universality and at the same time marks out the boundaries of the Church's earthly mission. And so eucharistic ecclesiology in no way rejects the universality of the Church but makes a distinction between exterior universality (in so far as the mission is limited), and interior universality which equals itself always and in all circumstances, because it means that the Church manifests itself everywhere, always in fullness and unity.' [22]

Thus the Church's fullness and unity are not a matter of quantity, but depend on the fullness and unity of the body of Christ, who is always and everywhere one and unique in His fullness. Christ is always the same, yesterday, to-day, and for ever, to one isolated church and to all the local churches as well. Eucharistic ecclesiology teaches that the unity and fullness of the Church attach to the notion of a local church, and not to the fluid and indefinite notion of the Universal Church. The Eucharist is where Christ dwells in the fullness of His Body: the Eucharist could never have been offered in a local church if it had been no more than one part of the Church of God. Where the Eucharist is, there is the fullness of the Church; *vice versa*, where the fullness of the Church is not, there no Eucharist can be celebrated. By denying the idea of 'parts,' eucharistic ecclesiology also excludes any concept of the Universal Church, for the Universal Church consists of parts, if it exists at all.

3. We have already noticed above that the concept 'Universal Church' carries with it the idea of primacy; that is to say, the Universal Church must have a single bishop at its head. This

---

[22] 'L'apôtre Pierre et l'évêque de Rome,' *Theologia*, Vol. XXVI, Athens, 1955, pp. 11–12.

'leadership' holds the reins of power over the Universal Church, although the leader is not above the Church but remains within its borders. An essential part of 'universalist' teaching must always be the building up of this power as a legal principle, in the Church, whether the power is absolute or limited. But now we come to a new question—does eucharistic ecclesiology carry with it an idea of primacy? If so, what will be its form and content?

Theologians were formerly interested in discussing whether the primitive local church had a single person as its Head (it hardly matters what name he was called by), or whether one-man management was a feature of the second stage in the history of Church organization. I cannot here deal with the historical side of the problem, and it is difficult to solve anyhow as direct information is lacking. But I would like to point out that, from an ecclesiological point of view, there can be no doubt that the local churches did have a single person as leader, from the very beginning. Eucharistic ecclesiology has its own pattern of thought, in which 'being Head of a local church' means 'being head' of the eucharistic assembly. The Last Supper was not the Eucharist, but only its institution. It became the Eucharist when Christ's disciples began to celebrate it in the breaking of bread and the blessing of the cup. Yet the Eucharist is not a repetition of the Supper: that, like the sacrifice on Golgotha, was accomplished 'once for all.' The Eucharist is a prolongation of the Supper in one special regard: it is an ecclesiological Last Supper, the 'feast of the Lord' celebrated in the Church, by whose celebration the Church has being. As in Jewish meals, which served as models for the Last Supper, so in the Eucharist one person must preside. On the day of Pentecost at Jerusalem the Eucharist was celebrated for the first time, and one of the disciples must have presided—it was certainly Peter. From that time onwards there was always one special person in the Eucharist, who broke the bread and blessed the cup. The head of the eucharistic assembly was also the head of the local church, that manifestation of the Church of God whose Head is Christ.

Who is leader of the multitude of churches, and how are they governed in actual fact? Would one local church, or perhaps its bishop, stand as head over all the rest? This sort of question makes us wonder if primacy can really exist in the Church alongside the thought-patterns of eucharistic ecclesiology. Before answering this, we must see what the multitude of local churches represents. If we were guided by our empirical consciousness, we should have been forced to picture this multitude as being in dispersion, since each local church was independent and autonomous. But the categories of empirical consciousness cannot apply in this matter. The multitude of local churches was *not* dispersed, it was united. The union was something absolutely *sui generis* : the unity was not the result of separate parts reuniting, but it was the unity of one and the same Church. Each local church united in itself all the local churches because it possessed all the fullness of the Church of God, and all the local churches together were united, because they were always this same Church of God. Though a local church did contain everything it needed within itself, it could not live apart from the other churches. It could not shut itself in or refuse to be acquainted with happenings in other churches : for anything that happened in other churches as well as its own, happened in the Church of God, the one and only Church. All the multitude of local churches forms one union founded on concord and love. Every local church must be in concord with all the other churches, because within the Church of God, ever one and only one, there can be no discord. This means, empirically speaking, that every local church accepts and makes its own anything that happens in other churches, and that all the churches accept everything that happens in each fellow-church. This acceptance (its regular designation is the word *reception* or *receptio*) is the witness of a local church indwelt by the Church of God, witnessing the work being done in other churches also indwelt by the Church of God : the Spirit bearing witness of the Spirit. By accepting what is being done in another church, one or several local churches bear witness that their actions are conformed to the will of God, and are therefore being done in the Church of God in Christ. Rejection of what is being done in a church, however, bears witness that such an action does not conform with the will of God.

The witness of local churches might vary in weight. Absolutely, every local church has the same value as another. This equality of value is between the Church of God and herself; for she is one, unique, and fully present in the eucharistic assembly of every local church. If the local churches were not equal in value, we should have to say that the Church of God was not equal to itself in value. But there is no need to think that equality of value between local churches destroys the hierarchy of these churches, far from it : the equality creates a hierarchy of churches grounded in the authority of witness belonging to the several local churches. The Church of God lives fully present in the eucharistic assembly of the local churches, but each of them has a different way and degree of making the presence actual in its own life. A local church will have higher authority of witness if it has a greater realization of the presence of the Church of God. Though the local churches are by nature equal in value, they are not necessarily equal in authority : this difference in authority causes hierarchy among them. If there is a hierarchy of churches, there must also be a church to head the hierarchy : therefore, a church that takes the first place. Its act of bearing witness to events in other churches has a sovereign value, and its act of 'reception' is of decisive importance. To put it another way; this church holds a two-fold priority, of authority and love, which means it makes a sacrificial gift of itself to the others. If the priority is of this nature we cannot possibly say that a church possessed of priority has *power* over the other churches. It never possessed or could possess power, for the power of a church having priority over the others would mean power over the Body of Christ. One cannot even say that the primacy was one of honour, for in ancient times the ideas of honour and power were associated together. What is more, there was nothing honorific about priority in the hierarchy of churches, in the modern sense of the word : the church that came first among the local churches won its place by services rendered, and not by prestige. It could not impose its will on the other churches or make them carry out its decisions, for all decisions must first be ratified by other local churches. Another point to notice : even in the period of ecumenical councils, and in spite of a system of Church order which was quite different from what it had been before Nicaea, even then no one church or group of churches had power over the others, in any strict sense of the word. If one of the churches did not recognize some doctrine as a manifestation of the will of God, no one could force it to do so. Even the imperial power, though it possessed the means to constrain, was often powerless in such matters. Thus it came about that one church gradually drew away from the main flock into a separate fold (by itself or with other churches who had the same

ideas), and this fold would be thought heretical or schismatic by
the other churches, because it had refused the witness of the church-
in-priority and of other churches in concord with the leading one.

The church-in-priority had no power, and no special rights
either: the many churches were not joined by law, but by love
and concord. That is why a single church surrounded by many
concordant churches only increases in authority by a corresponding
increase in love. The church that had priority naturally would be
possessed of the highest degree of authority, together with the
greatest love, and would always be ready to come to the help of
churches in need. Dionysius of Corinth says in a letter to Pope
Soter: 'Your custom [at Rome] has been from the beginning to
do good to your brethren in various ways, and send succour to
numerous churches in every city: thus, you have comforted the
nakedness of the indigent, and you have sustained our brethren
in the mines by the help you sent from the very first. You
[Romans] are keeping the old Roman tradition, which your blessed
Bishop Soter not only preserves but even enhances, by the abundant
provision and help that he sends to the saints, and also by consoling
the brethren who come to him with words of cheer, like a kind
father who loves to do his children good.' [23] The basis of priority
is neither power, nor honour, but only the authority that flows from
love and is made manifest by love. The church-in-priority may make
mistakes, in the very act of coming to the rescue of churches in
need and especially of churches in error; that is why the witness
of the other churches is needed. Its grand mistake is wanting to
impose a sovereign will or put itself above other churches. This is
the first step that leads in the end to revoking priority and resisting
the will of God, for it is a renouncing of the love that spreads all
over the Church. By putting itself above all the number of local
churches, which embosom its own priority, it takes a road that may
lead it outside the bounds of that number, to a place where there
is no priority, only a realm of 'ecclesiological vacuum.' Priority implies the existence of a number of local churches, and every church
among them is the Church of God just as much as the church-in-
priority is. When a local church invokes the church-in-priority, it
is not invoking judgment from a tribunal against which there is no
appeal; but coming to the church-in-priority so as to find itself, by
hearing the voice of the Church which dwells there.

[23] Eusebius, *Hist. Eccl.* iv, xxiii, 10.

A hierarchy of churches, based on authority of witness, implies that the churches which form the hierarchy and are led by the church-in-priority, all have full ecclesial *esse;* but it further implies that other churches will have priority in the smaller circles of local churches. This means that the church-in-priority possesses the highest authority, but not the sole authority; the other churches in their lower places in the hierarchy have their own authority, and neither kind excludes the other.

What possible explanation can we give for the priority of one church among the whole number of local churches? You may explain it, to be sure, by her own endeavours to manifest in her own life the Church of God in Christ, on the basis of purely historical facts; her being in some special town, or being founded by Apostles, or having many adherents : but all these causes are not enough in themselves, since other local churches may perfectly well possess whatever advantages the church-in-priority possesses. It must be admitted in the end that priority is a gift of God, and so an election by God. We cannot fully understand it, but the whole mass of local churches accept it in freedom and love, and follow the church-in-priority.

We may now return to a former enquiry : does the eucharistic type of ecclesiology include the idea of primacy, or not? After all we have said about it, clearly the only possible answer is negative : eucharistic ecclesiology excludes the idea of primacy by its very nature. As we already know, primacy means the power of one bishop over the whole universal Church. Such a power cannot exist in the eyes of eucharistic ecclesiology, or (to be exact) this power cannot pass beyond the bounds enclosing a local church. Conversely, as we have already seen, the local churches appear, to the eyes of eucharistic ecclesiology, not as separated or divided; not at all, they are mutually joined together. One of them occupies a very special position, and so finds itself Head of the other churches. In describing this state of affairs I prefer to use the word 'priority,' and not the word 'primacy.' Such a terminological nicety may seem very artificial, but it is justified because the concept of primacy is so enormously different from the concept of priority; indeed either concept almost excludes the other. In eucharistic ecclesiology, priority belongs to one of the local churches; but the concept of primacy, in its historical shape and setting, assumes that primacy belongs to one of the bishops, and that he governs the whole Church by established right. Consequently, primacy is a legalistic expression, whereas priority is founded on authority of witness, and that is a gift God grants to the church-in-priority. Of course the priority of a church is reflected in the person of its bishop, but eucharistic ecclesiology would think his priority was a secondary phenomenon; universal ecclesiology holds that a bishop's primacy is an essential phenomenon. Throughout history, the primacy of a bishop has always been tied to some definite church, but we may admit *theoretically* that the person who possesses primacy might be found altogether outside any definite church; certain trends in Catholic thought prove it. Finally, we should note that the two concepts imply different doctrines of Church unity: the 'primacy' school attributes the unity to the Church universal, while those who uphold 'priority' say that every local church has it. The difference between the concepts (primacy and priority) is very important: if you accept the idea of primacy you must ban eucharistic ecclesiology; conversely, accept priority and there is no room for universal ecclesiology.

4

1. As I said before, if people transpose the universal ecclesiology of to-day into a time before it existed, they will make an inaccurate picture of Church life in the ancient world. They will set problems unknown to that period, and unanswerable by our learning. For this reason I must now turn to consider a few historical facts in the light of eucharistic ecclesiology. In surveying the horizon of history, I hope, incidentally, to find a chance of showing that eucharistic ecclesiology is not an abstract theological speculation, unrelated to live reality, but can be evidenced from the Church's own history.

It will have to be a restricted historical analysis, partly because lack of space in the present work is a limitation, but even more because eucharistic ecclesiology gradually gave way to universal ecclesiology, from the second half of the third century onwards.

2. According to universal ecclesiology, the Church had a single personal Head, chosen by Christ as soon as its life began. Can we find a historical proof that such a person ever existed, and was he the Apostle Peter, as Catholic theologians assert? If the Apostle

Peter was not the leader of the Church, we are forced to conclude that the Catholic doctrine of primacy has no ecclesiological roots, was formed gradually in the course of history, and cannot therefore be regarded as a dogmatic obligation. A further question in this connection, still more important for Catholics, is the succession after Peter. If Peter had no successors, the whole doctrine of primacy would be undermined.

But we must also put yet another question: is the primacy of Peter a problem we can properly discuss? As a matter of fact, such a problem would never arise in the mind of the primitive Church. The first Christians were not concerned to discuss who was Head of the Church, or, in concrete terms, was Peter the Head or not; it was no problem to them because they had no need at all to ask this kind of question. The first Christians were as yet innocent of the very idea that there could be a power over the local churches, let alone discussing whether this power belonged to an individual, whether a Church or an Apostle, whether Jerusalem, Antioch, or Rome; it had never crossed their minds.

The primacy of Peter has its premises in the statement 'When Christ founded the Church, He had the Universal Church in view.' To say the least of it, the statement is scarcely capable of being demonstrated; furthermore, the whole Pauline doctrine of the Church is against it. Cyprian of Carthage was the first person who voiced the idea that Matt. 16: 17–19 is a text about the Universal Church. Admittedly we can find pointers to this *logion* of Christ as early as Justin (though he only comments on verse 17): [24] but neither Justin, nor Irenaeus, nor Tertullian so much as asked the question, or even wanted to know if the passage referred to the Universal Church: to them, the idea of a Universal Church was non-existent. Even granting that the statement is true; granting that Matt. 16: 18 ought to be taken to mean, that Christ promised to build His Church on Peter; does this mean that Christ has placed Peter at the head of 'His Church'? We cannot draw that conclusion, and would never have done so unless the idea of a Universal Church had been in our minds already. What is more, such a conclusion would make the *logion* itself appear a trifle illogical. If Peter really is the rock on which the Church is built, how can he

[24] J. Ludwig, *Die Primatworte Mt* xvi. 18, 19 *in der altkirchlichen Exegese*, Münster, W., p. 7.

be the chief of the Church at the same time? In so far as Peter is the rock on which the Church is built, his role is passive: the Church is built on Peter by Christ, not by Peter.[25] The only grounds for giving Peter power over the Church might be found in Christ's promise to give him 'the keys of the Kingdom of Heaven.' 'The keys,' of course, can be seen as a different thing from 'binding and loosing'; but in the *logion* itself the 'power of the keys' is not the point. We shall not find the promised 'power of the keys' in our *logion* unless, I repeat, we take our start from an assumed idea of the Universal Church.

We will now leave aside all the familiar difficulties that arise in interpreting Matt. 16: 18, and will allow that Christ made Peter head of the Church by these words. If this had been the case, then the primacy of Peter would certainly have become clear and manifest in the course of early Church history. Yet the relevant historical facts in this period are far from proving it so. There is a great deal we do not know about Apostolic times, but surely the Church's memory cannot have failed to preserve what was most important. A study of the Acts will provide us with one incontestable conclusion: Peter *was* head of the church of Jerusalem, which was a local church, although it was for a time the only church; when other local churches grew up, James, the brother of the Lord, became chief of the church of Jerusalem. We do not know if Peter was head of some other church at the time. In supporting the primacy of Peter, we should have to say that he exerted his primacy independently, without connection with any local church—a quite impossible assertion to make, either about those days or about any other. We see, then, that the primacy of Peter was not plainly manifested in the Primitive Church, and that we cannot positively assert the fulfilment of the promise given to Peter, at least not if we understand it as a promise of primacy. We are faced here with riddles that we are in no fit state to answer, and the reason for the riddles is that we stated the problem badly.

3. If we take eucharistic ecclesiology for our starting-point, many of the riddles can be answered without much trouble. In that case we must not ask whether Peter was head of the Church. The interesting question now is, which local church had the priority in that period; or rather, did any church have priority during the

[25] P. Bonnard, *Jésus-Christ édifiant son Eglise.* Neuchâtel and Paris, 1948, p. 26.

apostolic age? Eucharistic ecclesiology would seem to imply so. Apparently no one contests the special place held by the Church of Jerusalem until the death of James, brother of the Lord; it only remains to see what kind of place it held. Is Bishop Cassian right in his assertion that the Church of Jerusalem constituted the hierarchical centre during the primitive period, or anyhow until the city fell, and the other churches lived under its jurisdiction? [26] The phraseology does not matter, since the writer is speaking the language of convention. What we really want to know is whether the Church of Jerusalem had *power* over the others. In the time of famine, under the emperor Claudius, the Church of Antioch sent help to the Church of Jerusalem by the good offices of Barnabas and Saul (Acts 11: 30). Luke thought it his duty to record this, which was very likely the first occasion when one church sent help to another: the first, but not the last; the story of the ancient church abounds with similar examples. Whether or not the Church of Antioch was dependent on Jerusalem, this move of theirs was an expression of the love uniting all the churches. And no doubt they would have done the same for any other church that might have needed help. The Apostle Paul lays particular stress on collecting offerings for the poor, to benefit the Church of Jerusalem. This collection has been endlessly discussed by theological writers. It is very dubious—really utterly improbable—that Paul saw in it a sort of Christian 'two drachmae' payable to a Christian Jerusalem. Even if he did, we have still no reason to infer that the local churches, in Palestine or outside, thought themselves in any way subject to the power of the church at Jerusalem. It is common knowledge that the power of the Sanhedrin did not extend to the Jewish *diaspora;* its authority was purely of a moral and religious kind. Paul collected his contributions because the people were moved with a loving impulse, and a desire to help the needy, especially those of the Church of Jerusalem. Another point struck Paul even more strongly: he thought this piece of charity was a visible proof that the Jewish-Christian and Gentile-Christian churches were at one. The theological significance of these collections was therefore unquestionable.[27]

[26] Bishop Cassian 'Saint-Pierre et l'Eglise dans le Nouveau Testament (le problème de la Primauté),' *Istina*, 1955, No. 3, pp. 262–4.
[27] J. Munck, *Paulus und die Heilsgeschichte*, Copenhagen, 1954, pp. 286ff.

The facts I have just explained prove the special character of the place held by the Church of Jerusalem. To define this we must begin with the presuppositions that were accepted in the Apostolic Age, and set aside all modern assumptions. This brings us to the following definition: after local churches had grown up, in Palestine and also beyond its borders, the Church of Jerusalem had a prioritarian position among them. It possessed priority by virtue of being the church most authoritative in witnessing. This place of honour is easy to understand: from Pentecost onwards, Jerusalem was the first place where the Church of God in Christ had taken shape, and the building up of the local churches began from Jerusalem: there Christ suffered and rose again; there for some while they expected His second coming, and there was the dwelling-place of the Apostles. All this made a halo of special glory round Jerusalem, and the Jewish-Christians were not alone in seeing it, the Gentile Christians saw it too. There was no other church that could be compared to Jerusalem, and so its witness had the most authority. Any disagreement with Jerusalem amounted almost to deviation from the true faith, and agreement carried a corresponding guarantee of soundness. No wonder the Apostle Paul found it necessary to explain to Jerusalem what sort of Gospel he was preaching to the Gentiles; it was the only way he could find out if 'his race was run in vain' (Gal. 2: 2). His action was no sort of appeal to a higher court, a court possessed of the power to license or prohibit Paul's missionary activities. If the Church of Jerusalem had been a hierarchical centre, Paul would have needed to get his authorization in advance, a thing that he never dreamed of asking. When Paul applied to the Church of Jerusalem (repre-sented by 'those of most reputation') he wanted them to bear witness to the truth and authenticity of his gospel. Paul himself says nothing about his motives for doing this, and speaks only of a revelation: 'I went up [to Jerusalem] in obedience to a revelation and communicated unto them that gospel which I preach unto the Gentiles, but privately to them which were of reputation' (Gal. 2: 2). Nevertheless, if we are to be guided by what we find in the Acts, we could suppose that Paul applied to the Church of Jerusa-lem after, and because of, the conflict there had been at Antioch, when doubts had been expressed whether Paul's doctrine was the truth. Acceptance of his Gospel by the Church of Jerusalem gave witness that it was true. We can say, in short, that Paul applied to the church which possessed the greatest authority, and the Church of Jerusalem behaved like a church-with-priority.

Paul undoubtedly recognized that the Church of Jerusalem had supreme authority in matters of witness; but this recognition, to him, did not oblige him to feel dependent on the Church of Jerusalem in respect of his personal action, or in respect of the churches he had founded. When Paul looks back on his visits to Jerusalem in the epistle to the Galatians, he makes it clearly understood that he does not depend on the Church of Jerusalem in his apostolic activity. I think it is very unlikely that Paul believed he ought to go to Jerusalem in order to give them an account of his missionary journeys.[28] The visit spoken of in Gal. 2: 1–10 was inspired by other motives, as we know. As for his last journey to Jerusalem, all we know is that Paul wanted to deliver personally the assistance he had brought for their poor to the Church of Jerusalem.

The sources give us no reason to suppose that Paul was in a dependent relation to Jerusalem; and no ground either for asserting that the Church of Jerusalem ever claimed to extend her power over the Pauline churches or Paul himself. Whatever conflicts there were, if any, between Paul and the Church of Jerusalem, and particularly James, one thing is beyond question. There was a strong opposition-party within that Church, and it became stronger still after Paul's *concordat* with the 'Pillars' (Gal. 2: 9). If the Church of Jerusalem really had any power over Paul, the members of the opposition could have tried to obtain a clearly worded decision against him. Besides, the 'judaizers'—whether sent or not by James, or by the Church of Jerusalem—at any rate did not behave like people who have been given a definite mandate. When a church or a personage invests people with the power that a mission implies, they do not behave as the 'judaizers' did.[29] One further point must be added to these remarks, and it concerns ecclesiology. Even if Jerusalem had possessed universal jurisdiction, it could not have reached beyond the churches and their bishops; it could not cover individual Christians, who were dependent on their several

[28] Bishop Cassian, *art. cit.,* p. 263.
[29] The 'judaizers' were connected in various ways with the Church of Jerusalem; or perhaps we should follow Munck (op. cit.) in supposing that they were former Gentiles converted to Christianity.

churches; otherwise we should have to suppose that there were no
churches outside the Church of Jerusalem, and this was not the
case. Paul could not be dependent on the Church of Jerusalem; he
was never a member of it. As an apostle he could not be dependent
on the Church of Jerusalem, either; for his apostolate was, in his
own words 'not of men neither by man.' He was like the other
apostles in never being bishop of a church founded by himself.
The theory of the apostle-bishop, so widely accepted in Catholic
and even non-Catholic circles, is the product of theological speculation : the object is to prove that the monarchical episcopate was
there from the beginning. The primitive churches saw an *episcopus*
as presiding over a single local church, not a group. Paul was
admittedly the head-figure to the churches he founded; even so, he
cannot have been the *episcopus* of so many all at once.

It is just as bad ecclesiology to ask the question : was the
Apostle Peter dependent on the Church of Jerusalem? I confess
that, to me, the problem of Peter's primacy seems a false problem;
but the problem of Peter himself is real. I cannot possibly tackle
the subject at present, or I should wander too far from the immediate point under review. It is enough simply to say that Peter
stood in a place apart among the apostles, and his ministry was
unique in kind and had no later parallels. The apostle Peter is the
rock on which the Church is built, and will remain the rock until
the coming of the Lord. But Peter's place and his apostolic ministry
could never have set him outside the Church's boundaries. Another
thing to note : belonging in the Church is concrete, not abstract,
that is, you cannot belong in the Church in general, you have to
belong in one church in particular : the Church of God is manifested as empirical reality in the local churches. This concrete way
of belonging in a local church implies a relation of dependence
upon it, though we should be careful to avoid describing this
dependency in modern terms of law and jurisdiction, for grace is
its foundation. The dependence is really on the will of God, who
rules the Church's life. In the early days of the Church of
Jerusalem's life, the apostle Peter was its head; this did not
make him independent in regard to the Church, for in that case
he could not have functioned as its head. Conversely, the Church
of Jerusalem depended, to some extent, on Peter as being its head.
During this phase of Peter's life, his course of action had to run

parallel to the action of the Church of Jerusalem, in full concord. So there is no surprise in the fact that after his missionary journey and the conversion of Cornelius, Peter reported them to the Jerusalem church assembly. How could he possibly withhold such an amazing story from them: an uncircumcised pagan received into the Church (for the first time, according to the Acts)? When they heard these things (that is, after hearing Peter's account) they held their peace and glorified God, saying, 'Then to the Gentiles also, hath God granted repentance unto life' (Acts 11: 18). Here was an example of the Church of Jerusalem bearing witness about the will of God, and submitting (the Church, not Peter alone) to God's will. Legal submission (i.e. to a qualified authority) belongs to quite a different world, and Luke's story makes no mention of it. We know almost nothing about St. Peter's doings after he left Jerusalem; but we can state as a high probability that, whatever St. Peter was doing, he was not dependent on the Church of Jerusalem, anyhow in a legalistic sense, and least of all as an apostle of Christ. If he had been dependent, we should have had to ask how and where his dependency could find concrete expression. After the 'Apostolic Council' which Peter attended, as the Acts tell, he never came to Jerusalem again, so he cannot have participated in the Jerusalem church assembly. We are left with the supposition—most unlikely—that Peter sent in regular reports to Jerusalem. Still another hypothesis is suggested by O. Cullmann in his book on St. Peter: that Peter was dependent not on the Church of Jerusalem but on St. James in person because he was the head of the Christian-Jewish mission.[30] This notion rests on the supposition that St. James was actually the head of the Universal Church. But that is a highly questionable hypothesis, without any *data* in its support; and it led O. Cullmann to the conclusion that the Christian Jews, no matter where they might be situated, were always dependent on St. Peter. According to O. Cullmann, in one self-same church, says the Church of Rome, some of the faithful were dependents of St. Peter, and others looked elsewhere. Such a supposition is quite inadmissible, because it leaves out the idea of the Church.

4. After James died, and still more after Jerusalem fell in A.D. 70, the Church of Jerusalem ceased to play the part of leading church. It disappeared from the historical stage: when it

---

[30] O. Cullmann, op. cit., pp. 37, 39.

made a new entrance it appeared as a little church in the new pagan city of Aelia Capitolina, and the congregation were entirely composed of Gentile Christians. So far had its prestige crumbled, that even in Palestine leadership had passed to the Church of Caesarea; surely this is still further proof that the Church of Jerusalem had not held the primacy before the year 70. Primacy in any case is inseparably bound up with a man, not with a church. If the primacy belonged to James, he would have passed it over to his successors; men δεσπόσυνοι like himself, that is, kindred of Christ in the flesh. To whom, then, was the priority transferred which formerly belonged to the Church of Jerusalem? The New Testament scriptures give us no guidance on this point, and so we have to look for an answer in the facts of history, and the premises of ecclesiology. If the local churches were gathered round one authoritative church in the beginning, why were they to do without such a centre later on? We can strongly assert that no church could have inherited Jerusalem's authority in full. The authority given to the Church of Jerusalem was unique and unrepeatable. True enough; but there is no need to ask whether another church could have inherited Jerusalem's authority in full. We are only concerned to discover which had *most* authority among the churches; if not so great as the primitive authority of Jerusalem, anyhow greater than the others could boast.

Let us turn to the facts. We know that the Church of Rome took over the position of 'Church-with-priority' at the end of the first century. That was about the time when her star ascended into the firmament of history in its brightest splendour. We cannot tell exactly when this happened, for there was never a formal transmission of priority from Jerusalem to Rome. Even as early as the epistle to the Romans, Rome seems to have stood out among all the churches as a very important one. Paul bears witness that the faith of the Romans was proclaimed throughout the whole world (Rom. 1: 8). The persecutions of Nero did not reduce the Church of Rome to nothing, but it was so badly damaged that some lapse of time was needed to arouse its spirit and collect its numerical strength. In the time of this transition, as we should expect, it could not play the part of leading church. We do not know who held the priority during this comparatively short period: it may possibly have been Antioch, which stood in an important ecclesiastical position even in the time of St. James. It may have been Ephesus, though it is less likely, for that church's influence never spread beyond Asia Minor. If Ephesus had really possessed the priority then, surely it would have had possession at the end of the first century. However, we have a document, which gives us our earliest reliable evidence that the Church of Rome stood in an exceptional position of authority in this period. This is the epistle of Clement of Rome. Modern theological scholars (especially the Protestant sort) regard Clement of Rome as a name intimately associated with the beginnings of pre-Catholicism, or even of Catholicism at Rome. This is one of the great formulas to be found in modern theological learning, those formulas potent as magic spells, even when totally groundless. We know that Clement was 'president' of the Roman Church: that is all. G. Dix, writing to defend the theory of apostle-bishops, considered that Clement was the heir and successor of the apostles Peter and Paul in exactly the same way as (he thinks) Timothy and Titus had been. In other words, Clement is supposed to have been the bishop of a considerable number of churches, which were governed by presbyteries. This opinion belongs in a world of pure fantasy, and will not stand up to serious critical investigation.[31]

The epistle is not written by Clement alone; but in the name of the Roman Church. 'The Church of God dwelling in Rome to the Church of God dwelling in Corinth.' This form of address already proves that the Roman Church did not set itself above the Church of Corinth; they are both called 'Church of God.' There is no hint in the epistle of any claim being made by the Church of Rome to exercise any power over the Church of Corinth. If the Church of Rome had believed itself to be invested with a higher power, then the Epistle of Clement would surely have been written in a very different tone. We do not know exactly what had happened at Corinth; the epistle only mentions a 'rebellion' against the presbyters, which had led to the presbyters (or rather, one presbyter) being ejected. This presbyter was the head of the Church, that is he was the bishop. We again do not know by what means the news of these events had reached Rome. It is easy to suppose that the presbyter or presbyters thus ejected applied to the Church

[31] G. Dix, 'The Ministry in the Early Church,' in *The Apostolic Ministry,* 1946, pp. 253–66.

of Rome. But could they have thought Rome had the power to annul their ejection? This is most unlikely; the establishment or ejection of presbyters was the business of a local church. The real reason they applied to the Roman Church was that Rome might refuse to recognize the recent decisions made in the Church of Corinth; might refuse *receptio* of what had taken place in the Church of Corinth. The Church of Rome did that very thing: bore witness that the ejected presbyters had done nothing amiss, and said that their deposition was not in accordance with the will of God. This was not Rome laying down the law, but the Church bearing witness on what had happened within the Church. The epistle is couched in very measured terms, in the form of an exhortation; but at the same time clearly shows that the Church of Rome was aware of the decisive weight that must attach to its witness about the events in Corinth, in the Church of Corinth's eyes. So the Church of Rome, at the end of the first century, exhibits a marked sense of its own priority, in point of witness about events in other churches. Note also that the Roman Church did not feel obliged to make a case, however argued, to justify its authoritative pronouncements on what we should now call the inside concerns of other churches. There is nothing said about the grounds of this priority; even though the text of the epistle mentions the apostles Peter and Paul and their death under Nero's persecution, and one might well expect this to have been enlarged upon as affording a foundation for Roman priority. Apparently Rome had no doubt of having its priority accepted without argument. The only apology made is for not having sent a letter earlier to the Church of Corinth, so as to restore order there; the delay being due to persecutions.

5. We do not know if the Corinthian Church followed Rome's advice, but we may fairly suppose that the voice of the Roman Church made itself heard. Anyhow, Clement's epistle was held in high esteem at Corinth thereafter. This is an interesting fact, but it still does not prove that Rome's priority was recognized by other churches. Our next task, therefore, is to find out what the views of other churches were. We find the first direct evidence about the priority of the Roman Church in Ignatius of Antioch. Speaking of the Church of Rome, Ignatius uses the phrase 'which presides' in two passages. 'Ignatius also named Theophoros . . .

to the church which presides in the land of the Romans . . . which presides in (the) Charity (ἀγάπη).'[32] The term *agape* is the hardest part of the passage to explain, but the difficulty vanishes if we take account of the special meaning Ignatius gave to *agape*: for him, *agape* meant 'the local church in its eucharistic aspect.' Each local church is *agape*: all local churches together are also *agape*, because each local church, says Ignatius, is the Catholic Church and so manifests the Church of God in Christ. In the empirical sphere, however, the churches form a union based on charity, and this union may also be spoken of in the same words. The Roman Church 'presides' in love, that is, in the concord based on love between all the local churches. The term 'which presides' (προκαθημένη) needs no discussion; used in the masculine it means the bishop, for he, as head of the local church, sits in the 'first place' at the eucharistic assembly, that is, in the central seat. He is truly the president of his church. Because a local church was by nature identical with the concord of all the churches in love, an image came naturally to Ignatius's mind: he pictured the local churches grouped, as it were, in a eucharistic assembly, with every church in its special place, and the Church of Rome in the chair, sitting in the 'first place.' So, says Ignatius, the Church of Rome indeed has the priority in the whole company of churches united by concord. We are not told by Ignatius (or Clement either) why the Church of Rome should preside, and not some other church. To Ignatius it must have seemed self-evident, and proofs a waste of time. In his period no other church laid claim to the role, which belonged to the Church of Rome. In the beginning of the second century, the Church of Alexandria had not yet appeared on the historical scene, but seemed to lurk in some mysterious shadow. As for the Church of Ephesus—Ignatius did indeed give them an epistle, but it does not contain the least allusion to their having any special role. The only important church after Rome was Antioch—they could have claimed leadership—but Ignatius himself attributes this part to Rome, although he is quite clear that great respect is due to his own church and to himself. It is enough to compare his epistle to the Church of Rome with the other Ignatian epistles; one immediately feels the difference of tone. In his other

---

[32] Romans. Salutation. Ignatius of Antioch, *Letters*, tr. P. T. Camelot in *Sources chrétiennes* 10, Paris, 1951, p. 125.

epistles he teaches like a doctor, but when addressing Rome, he will not venture to give any advice at all. Every line in this epistle is charged with special deference to 'the Church that presides in Love.'

Nevertheless, in the epistle to the Church of Rome, we find no reference to its power over the other churches, and Ignatius does not say anything about the Bishop of Rome. This is puzzling to us, but also proves that Ignatius had absolutely no idea of Roman primacy. Priority, to him, did not imply the notion of power. Priority must, of course, be so understood as to correspond with the way in which the local churches are understood. If every church's life is founded on love, if love underlies all relations with other churches, then priority too must spring from love, and be a living example of love's authority. Ignatius almost certainly knew Clement of Rome's epistle, in which the Church of Rome refused to countenance the ejection of Corinthian presbyters; but he had never heard of any standards laid down by the Church of Rome to regulate doctrine or discipline. If such standards existed, he would certainly have applied them to various issues, especially to his doctrine of bishops. He writes to the Romans 'As for you, you have been grudging to none, you have taught others. I can only wish that what you enjoin on others by your instructions may carry due weight.' [33] But the words are used in a very limited sense. The reference is solely to moral issues; and here especially to envy, which had been the chief subject of Clement's epistle.

Ignatius, in another saying even harder to explain, says that the Church of Rome 'presides in the region of the Romans' ($\pi\rho o\kappa a\theta\tilde{\eta}\tau a\iota$ $\dot{\epsilon}\nu$ $\tau\dot{o}\pi\omega$ $\chi\omega\rho\dot{\iota}o\upsilon$ $\mathrm{P}\omega\mu a\dot{\iota}\omega\nu$). What does this mean? We can be sure Ignatius was not talking here about the Roman Church presiding in Rome itself, for such an expression would be meaningless: a bishop can preside over a church, but a church cannot preside over itself. We must therefore suppose that Ignatius is talking about the Church of Rome's presidency among the local churches, situated 'in Roman country.' We do not know what churches these were, but it is an established fact that other churches in central Italy did exist in the time of Ignatius. His words justify us in supposing some kind of union between various Italian local churches; among them the Roman Church possessed the priority.

[33] Rom. 3 : 1.

If so, a further conclusion may be drawn: in the period of Ignatius of Antioch, besides the one great union of all local churches, more limited unions had come into being, groups of churches round one particular church which had the most authority. Such unions had arisen through the force of events. After all, it was not always either easy or essential to invoke Rome, with her then supreme priority. It was much simpler and more convenient to approach some less distant church, possessed of greater authority than her neighbours. Ecclesiastical hierarchy had always been there, ever since the churches first began. The church-in-priority certainly had authority, but this did not prevent a daughter-church from also having an authoritative position among churches less than itself, only, of course, its authority could not be so great. Ignatius regards Rome as the church-in-priority, and his witness on this point agrees with the Roman Church's self-witness, as we find it in the epistle of Clement.

6. We shall find other evidence about the Roman position, in Irenaeus, Bishop of Lyons. His *Adversus Haereses* contains a famous passage, which has provoked a great many arguments. This is unquestionably the most important document of all, with regard to the position of the Roman Church; the author is a father of the Church in the second half of the second century, a man who enjoyed a very high prestige. The passage has come down to us in a Latin translation, and this makes it difficult to interpret in many places. I have chosen to quote the Latin because there is, so far, no translation generally accepted. *Ad hanc enim ecclesiam propter potentiorem principalitatem necesse est omnem convenire ecclesiam, hoc est eos qui sunt undique fideles, in qua semper ab his qui sunt undique conservata est ea quae est ab apostolis traditio.*[34] This sentence has been discussed for centuries, almost word by word; but the most important point has never been discussed at all; nobody has asked whether Irenaeus was here talking about the Church of *Rome*. In other words, does the exordium *ad hanc enim ecclesiam* point to the Church of Rome? Till now all theologians,

[34] The French translation proposed by F. Sagnard (*Irénée de Lyon, contre les Hérésées,* 'Sources chrétiennes,' No. 54, I, III, Paris, 1952) runs: 'This Church (of Rome), by reason of being founded with more powerful authority, must command the concordance of every church with herself: that is, of the faithful who come from everywhere: she in whom THE TRADITION, coming from the Apostles, has always been preserved, by those who come from everywhere.'

of every confession and trend, have agreed on assuming that the church in question was undoubtedly Rome. But Pierre Nautin broke this *consensus* up quite recently in his important article: 'Irenaeus, *Adv. Haer.* III, 3, 2. Church of Rome or Church Universal.' [35] In his opinion Irenaeus is not talking about the Church of Rome, far from it; he meant the Church Universal. A very original point of view this—even paradoxical. That a viewpoint is paradoxical, does not necessarily commend it to our favour; but neither does it prove the viewpoint is wrong, for truth often wears the guise of paradox, even in the field of theological inquiry. P. Nautin's article is very interesting, not only for its main thesis, which may be accepted or rejected as we please; but for the many fascinating observations it contains. I cannot of course linger over details now, but I must make up my mind for or against Nautin's main thesis. If he is right and the passage in *Adv. Haer.* III, 2, 3, has nothing to do with the Church of Rome, then it has no further interest for me. And the remarkable thing is that the author of the article himself comes to the same conclusion; the famous passage loses its former importance to scholars, under the light of his interpretation; a platitudinous truth is now seen to be its content, i.e. every church should be in accord with the Church Universal.

Nautin's fundamental premises, which prove his interpretation of *Adv. Haer.* III, 3, 2 right or wrong, lie in the assertion that Irenaeus's ecclesiology was 'universal.' If this universal type of ecclesiology had not yet come into being in Irenaeus's time, Nautin's interpretation simply disintegrates; Irenaeus cannot have been talking about the Universal Church if the idea was foreign to his thought. Readers of the article might find all the arguments convincing, if only Nautin had given really clear proof that this idea of a Universal Church was in Irenaeus's mind from the start. We find no such proof in his article; he never even raises the question of what ecclesiology Irenaeus believed.

Let us suppose Nautin was right, and that the idea of a Universal Church can really be found in Irenaeus. If so the sentence in question is no longer important and, worse still, the whole structure of Irenaeus's argument suffers the same fate. Irenaeus calls on apostolic tradition to correct the mistaken heretics. This tradition, he

---

[35] In *Revue de l'histoire des religions,* CLI 1, January-March 1957.

says, is guarded in every local church by the succession of bishops.[35a]
It was not in his power to find proof of this in each local
church, so he confines himself to one set of bishops only, and
enumerates the bishops of Rome, a church in which apostolic
tradition and the faith proclaimed to mankind have been guarded,
up to our own times. This should be enough to confound the setters
up of irregular conventicles. This is the reason (says Nautin) why
all churches, including those in heresy, must be in accord with the
Universal Church, if they claim really to be churches. But if
Irenaeus is truly discussing the Universal Church, how could he
suppose that accord with it would seem to the heretics an argument against their own heterodoxy—or an argument to the
faithful proving the apostolic tradition was true? What does
'being in accord with the Universal Church' really mean? When
we and our contemporaries say, and we often do, that the faithful
should be in accord with the Church, we surely mean in accord
with the doctrine preserved by the Church, as characterized and
expressed in the symbols of the Faith, the decisions of ecumenical
councils, the writings of the Church's fathers and the liturgical
life. None of these things were there in the second century (or
almost none); only the Scripture and the tradition were preserved
in each local church by the good offices of successive bishops.
In the second century, to insist on accord with the Universal
Church as a necessity is simply to pass from concrete to abstract:
the concept of the Universal Church is itself an abstraction. Finally
and essentially, any arguments against heretics based on the concept
of the Universal Church really involve accepting the heretical attitude. The heretics could always reply that *their* doctrine was right
and in accord with 'the Church,' that is, with the aeon 'ecclesia'
in their system of emanations. As for their attitude to Scripture
and Tradition—go back to Irenaeus's own words: 'When we con-
vict them by Scriptural proofs, they turn their attack upon the very
Scriptures. . . . Again, when we appeal to the Tradition, which
comes from the Apostles, and is kept in the churches by the succes-
sions of presbyters, they reject that Tradition' (III, II, 1–2).
Irenaeus leaves no room for the opinion of P. Nautin; for if his
sentence is taken to refer to the Universal Church, then it will
appear absolutely isolated from its context.

I must confess that P. Nautin's arguments do not convince me.

[35a] *Adv. haer.*, III, 3, 1.

It seems to me that Irenaeus *was* referring to the Church of Rome in *Adv. Haer.* III, 3, 2, and that there can be no argument about this. I admit that some of his expressions remain a little obscure to us, and our interpretations are just hypotheses, some plausible and others not. But the general sense of the sentence is clear enough, at least for my own purposes.[36] As I showed above, Irenaeus believed he could confine himself to enumerating the succession in a single church, viz. the Roman Church, although he might have enumerated the successive bishops in every local church, as he says himself. He gives his own explanation for choosing the Church of Rome: he saw it as 'the very great and the very ancient church, known to all, which the two most glorious apostles Peter and Paul founded and constituted.'[37] This last remark must have had some special value to Irenaeus, we suppose; to us it is rather disconcerting. No doubt Irenaeus knew some things about the foundation of the Roman Church which we do not know to-day. In any case, if we take the Latin text as our starting-point, we cannot draw the conclusion that Irenaeus thought that the Church of Rome was founded and constituted by Peter and Paul simultaneously. There is a strong possibility that the Latin translator brought together, in his translation, two actions which were separate in the mind of Irenaeus: namely, the foundation and the constitution of the Church at Rome. 'In it,' he goes on, 'the Apostolic Tradition was preserved by the succession of bishops.' A little before, Irenaeus insists that any one looking for the truth can find it in the Tradition of the Apostles, which every local church has preserved. So we must suppose he thought that the Apostolic Tradition and the Faith proclaimed to mankind were preserved in the Roman Church more fully than in others, or, at least, in a more manifest way. Later Irenaeus points to this Church—Rome—as the one to which all

---

[36] I cannot here give a philological analysis of Irenaeus's sentence, not only because space is lacking. In fact, philological analysis of the sentence has so far given us nothing, and any future yield is doubtful. Turning the Latin back into Greek would be a hopeful line if one had a dictionary of Irenaeus's works. But in proposing our different translations, we shall never be sure that the initial text has really been reconstructed. The translator of Irenaeus had a poor knowledge of Greek, or could not put Irenaeus's ideas into Latin; but he still had a great advantage over us: he had the original text before him, whereas all we have is a translation. We at most can find a Greek equivalent to a set of Latin words: we cannot be sure that these are exactly the words used by Irenaeus.

[37] P. Nautin, *art. cit.,* pp. 55–6.

other churches must *convenire*. Nautin, like most of his predecessors, thinks that the verb *convenire* means 'to be in agreement or accord.' But this is not the only meaning. I think a likelier sense of *convenire* here is 'address one's self to,' 'turn to,' 'have recourse to.' The sense of the remark would then be: every local church should have recourse to the Church of Rome. Irenaeus himself confirms this sense of *convenire* (*Adv. Haer.* III., 4, 1) in explaining what he had said about the Church of Rome: 'If at any time some simple question of detail should happen to provoke a dispute, surely the oldest churches, and those in which the Apostles lived, are the ones we should have recourse to (*recurrere*) and they will give us something very certain, and very clear, on the case in question.' This passage in Irenaeus illuminates the meaning of his remarks about the Church of Rome: if there are disputes in a local church, that church should have recourse to the Roman Church, for there is contained the Tradition which is preserved by all the churches.

The two meanings of *convenire*—accordance and recourse—are near but not identical. 'Being in accord' would mean that the Church of Rome can declare the norms, like edicts, with regard to faith and church discipline equally; and that the other churches must be in accord with these norms—in fact, they must accept them. This sense does not fit the context here, nor does it agree with what we know about the Church of Rome in the pre-Nicene period. The Church of Rome did not then initiate any decisions in the realm of Faith, or of discipline either. Rome's vocation consisted in playing the part of arbiter, and settling contentious issues by witnessing to the truth or falsity of whatever doctrine was put before them. Rome was truly the centre where all converged, if they wanted their doctrine to be accepted by the conscience of the Church. They could not count upon success except on one condition—that the Church of Rome had received their doctrine—and refusal from Rome predetermined the attitude the other churches would adopt. There are numerous cases of this recourse to Rome, but I will quote only one. According to Tertullian's story, Praxeas had managed to sway Pope Victor (or Zephyrinus) to condemn Montanism, and had also predisposed him, to some extent, in favour of monarchianism. In the treatise *Against Praxeas*, Tertullian's irritable feelings towards Rome are plain to the reader; he says that Praxeas has crucified the Father and driven away the

Paraclete. Praxeas obviously cannot have done this all by himself, and Tertullian's object of attack was not him, but the Church of Rome, which is accused of doing it for him. The Montanist Tertullian expresses the utmost dislike for 'the great church,' but he also understood very well that Rome's place and value were to be reckoned with: in his own words, Rome was the church *unde nobis quoque auctoritas praesto est.* This does not mean that the Church of Rome never settled any internal dogmatic question on its own initiative, as other Churches did; but generally the Roman bishops, in this period, preferred not to be involved in the dogmatic disputes going on at Rome; when they did interfere, it was often an unlucky move.

Let us return to the text of Irenaeus. He says that every local church, if contentious problems arise, must (*necesse*) have recourse to the Church of Rome. *Necesse* in Irenaeus does not suggest any legal obligation. The necessity springs from a more inward duty, reflecting the very nature of the church: the duty of appealing, if there is disagreement, to the church which has the greatest authority. This church bore her witness on events in the other churches; or perhaps it would be more accurate to say, events in the Church. The witness was not a verdict backed by the force of law, and, as such, constraining the other churches to obey. It was a free act when the local churches followed Rome's witness; they were accepting witness from a fellow-church because of its higher authority. But Rome's witness was not less valid, but a higher validity than any and every legal verdict. If there has ever been a time, in church history, when the catch-word *Roma locuta, causa finita* stood for something real, that time was before the Church of Rome had any powers by law.

As Irenaeus saw things, the necessity of appealing to the Church of Rome was based on its *potentior principalitas.* What does this expression mean? Perhaps one day the relevant line from Irenaeus will be discovered in a Greek text; that would be the only chance of finding an answer to our question, and an answer acceptable to all.[38] We have not been lucky enough to find it yet, so we must be content with hypotheses for the present. There has been some progress recently made in interpreting Irenaeus's phraseology. Fewer and fewer defenders can be found for the view than Irenaeus

[38] See the analysis of the different meanings of *potentior principalitas* in F. Sagnard's *Irénée de Lyon, contre les Hérésées,* pp. 414ff.

means, by *potentior principalitas,* 'primacy' of the Church of Rome, in the present-day sense. We should note that F. Sagnard, in his translation of the Third Book of *Adv. Haer.,* renders *'propter potentiorem principalitatem'* as 'by reason of the more powerful authority of its foundation.' This may not be altogether exact, but he seems right to me in thinking that Irenaeus was talking about authority rather than power. But since, in the first place, we have no hope of finding the meaning of Irenaeus's word by the method of philological analysis, and in the second place, we cannot find the exact Greek equivalent, the problem seems to me only soluble if we start from Irenaeus's characteristic ideas. He was wont to say 'The Church of Rome is the very great, very ancient church, known to all others, and founded and constituted by Peter and by Paul.' Might not *potentior principalitas* be simply an expression to describe Rome's particular position thus conceived? This church possesses the greatest authority among the churches; consequently it is the church with the priority. Surely, then, we could rightly say that the phrase *potentior principalitas* means 'priority'; this would correspond with the Greek ἀρχαιότης. The fact that this is the *greatest* priority shows that it is not the only one, and therefore does not exclude the priority of other churches in the more limited circles of local churches. Irenaeus had said himself, as we know, that litigious questions might be referred to churches founded by apostles, such as Smyrna and Ephesus.

The language of Irenaeus, as thus interpreted, excludes the idea of Roman primacy. Dom B. Botte has rightly pointed out that Irenaeus was not the man who formulated primacy.[39] One might say, however, that he was the formulator of Roman priority among all local churches whatsoever. The tone of Irenaeus echoes Ignatius when he describes the particular position in which Rome stood, and which no other church shared. 'Presiding in Love' in Ignatius corresponds with the *potentior principalitas* in Irenaeus. Irenaeus also agrees with Ignatius in his recognition that certain churches have their own priority, in the more limited circles of local churches. Irenaeus, like Ignatius, bears witness to the attitude of local churches concerning the Church of Rome, and we can be quite sure that their two witnesses were identical with the way the Roman

---

[39] Dom B. Botte, 'A propos de *l'Adversus Haereses* III, 3, 2, de saint Irénée' *Irenikon,* t. XXX (1957), No. 2, p. 162.

Church, itself, viewed its own position. Thus, to Clement, on the one hand, and Ignatius and Irenaeus on the other, the priority enjoyed by the Roman Church was due to authority of witness: or, to use more modern language, it possessed priority of *receptio*. The Church of Rome had a special position, and this was not only the result of its actual status in fact; it also implied having a very definite ecclesiological system, which said that each local church was the Church of God in all its fullness. This system is what I called eucharistic ecclesiology. Having made this analysis, I find one question still to be answered: to what extent did the Church of Rome, and its bishops especially, act in accordance with their position, as I have explained it above?

7. I have already mentioned Clement of Rome and his way of understanding the position of the Church of Rome. Clement was obviously a man of mark, and his epistle to the Corinthians is an extremely important document; but his action still fails to supply an answer to the question we raised above; in his time the Church of Rome had only recently taken cognizance of its prioritarian position. I have not room here to give an account of the history of the Roman Church in the pre-Nicene period; nor is it, indeed, called for. We know too little about some of the Roman bishops at that time; we cannot form an idea of how they regarded the position of the Roman Church; so I will be content to sketch the characters of two of these men, who are its most striking representatives; Pope Victor (189–198) and Pope Stephen (254–257).

Pope Victor, like Pope Stephen, has his place among the greatest men of action in the Roman Church. Some say, or rather insist, that Victor was the first Pope of Rome. This question—was Victor the first pope or not—is matter for much discussion; but one thing is beyond doubt, that Victor, like Stephen, was an extremely colourful personality, a most commanding figure. Nobody in the pre-Nicene period acted like these two; but does this justify the conclusion that they understood the position of Rome in a different way from Irenaeus? Their own characters might suffice to make them to act as they did, while yet remaining within the ancient ideological framework of priority. They were not alone in acting energetically. Did Cyprian act with less energy than Stephen? John Chrysostom, too, and Basil the Great showed great energy in action, yet nobody is going to say that they were the first popes of the

Orient. Why then should we take Victor's energetic action as grounds for thinking him the first Pope of Rome?

When people speak of Victor as the first Pope, they have in mind his action during the Paschal controversies. In these controversies, many things still remain obscured from our sight. We do not really know why Victor raised the Paschal question; did it arise from a domestic situation inside the Roman Church, or was it first raised by the churches of Asia Minor? Eusebius (our only source) did not pass Victor's epistle down to us, which is strange, considering that he included the epistle of Polycrates in his History. We must not forget that when Victor addressed the churches of Asia Minor, with a peremptory demand (if it was), he did so at a time when he had the backing of a virtual majority of churches. This peremptory demand surely means just that the Church of Rome had refused to accept the practice of Asia Minor. The churches of Asia Minor stood in isolation, since nearly all the other local churches had followed Victor's lead. Let us avoid the common mistake of talking about the churches of Asia Minor being 'excommunicated.' At the end of the second century, nobody thought it possible for one church to excommunicate another; nothing could be at issue beyond a breaking of brotherly communion between the churches. In his epistle to Victor, Irenaeus blames him for refusing to act in the gentle way of the presbyters, his predecessors; he did not accuse Victor of grasping special *power* over the Church for himself. Victor's behaviour was still within the bounds of ordinary ecclesiastical practice. If Victor had ventured to go further than any one before him, the fact is easily explained by his character. Apparently he was of African origin; and in Carthage at this period there was a sort of Christian cult of Rome. We have only to recall the dithyrambic praise of Rome, which we find in Tertullian's *De praescriptione haereticorum*. We simply have no *data* to justify the assertion that Victor, assuming the concept of the Universal Church, took the situation of the Roman Church to mean primacy of power.

As for Pope Stephen—has history treated him quite fairly? We nearly all start with a preconceived idea that, in the battle between him and Cyprian, Cyprian was right, and 'the tyrant' (as Cyprian had called Stephen) was wrong. Did Stephen base his actions on a new ecclesiastical ideology, and did Cyprian keep to tradition?

It would be more exact to say that neither of them kept to the traditional idea altogether, and that Cyprian had less respect for it than Stephen. Cyprian was possibly right in the case of the Spanish bishops, Basilides and Martial, but Stephen's behaviour was perfectly in keeping with the prioritarian role which the Roman Church had to play. The principle of priority needed no modification to allow of his granting the pleas of the Spanish bishops. In Clement's time the Corinthian presbyters had appealed to Rome with the same purpose, that is, to ask that no act of *receptio* should be made concerning the recent events in Corinth. Any church and any church member could appeal (*convenire* was Irenaeus's word) to any other church, and specially to the church-in-priority. Cyprian asserts that the Spanish bishops were reinstated by Stephen.[40] But here we surely have something more like Cyprian's own interpretation. Stephen had refused to recognize the eviction of the Spanish bishops, and consequently the setting-up of new bishops in their place was also not countenanced. In other words, there was no *receptio* for this act. Stephen's behaviour was perfectly natural and in this case especially because Spain was in the direct sphere of Roman influence, not of Carthaginian. The Spanish churches, according to Cyprian, appealed to Carthage (that is, to the Carthaginian council of bishops) for comfort and help. The Carthaginian Church could have taken its own line and kept Rome informed, pointing out that Basilides had led Stephen into error. Cyprian did nothing of the sort. The Council, of which he was president, decided that the new bishops had been regularly established, and that their establishment could not be made invalid because their predecessors were improperly re-established by Stephen. Even if Stephen's actions went beyond the limited scope which the Roman Church's priority allowed him—if, that is, he really did make the decision to re-establish the evicted bishops— Cyprian's action was none-the-less an innovation. He opposed the witness of the church-in-priority by the decisions of his council, and claimed for the council's decrees the force of law.

We will turn next to the baptismal controversies. I admit the great difficulty of forming an objective opinion, about the actions of the two antagonists. Stephen's epistle has reached us through the comments made on it by Cyprian and Firmilian of Caesarea,

[40] Epist. LXVII, V, 3.

both his enemies. Do their epistles give us the content of Stephen's epistle in a fair and exact way? It should be noted that the Latin text of Firmilian's epistle, found in the epistles of Cyprian, is not really a translation, but an adaptation from Firmilian's Greek original text: Cyprian wanted propaganda against Rome and adapted the text to suit his own angle.[41] This is why we cannot base our theories entirely on Firmilian's epistle. One further note; the question about the baptism of heretics and schismatics was not raised by Stephen in the first place: Cyprian started it, having for years pressed all churches, including Rome, to accept the practice of Carthage in this matter. Cyprian, supported on this point by the Councils of Carthage, did indeed reserve the right of every bishop to act as he saw fit, on the one condition of answering for his actions before God; but in fact he allowed no objections to stand in his way. Cyprian saw it not as an administrative problem, but as the *regula catholica*. A refusal to follow Cyprian's principles would indeed have created enormous practical difficulties. Imagine the case of a heretic—especially a Novatian—enrolled in the Church by Rome and then migrating to Carthage. How would Cyprian have acted? In his eyes such a person had not received baptism.

Stephen flatly refused to follow Cyprian concerning the baptism of heretics. Is his refusal evidence that Stephen believed Rome's situation, and his own, to depend upon the notion of primacy and power? Why indeed *should* Stephen have followed Cyprian's line about the baptism of heretics when the Church of Rome had a different practice from that which Cyprian commended? Cyprian's extraordinary insistence shows that he, and not Stephen, was trying to exercise some sort of leadership over the whole Church by means of his councils. Stephen probably was first in citing the *logion* in Matt. 16: 18. But Cyprian drove him to do so. Had not Cyprian first sent to Rome his treatise *De Unitate Ecclesiae*, which uses the magic words *cathedra Petri*? Had he not written that whoever deserts 'Peter's Chair' is putting himself outside the Church automatically? Had he not told Cornelius in his letter that Rome was *cathedra Petri et ecclesia principalis unde unitas sacerdotalis exorta*

---

[41] See J. Ludwig, *Die Primatworte Mt. XVI*, 18, 19, *in der altkirchlicher Exegese* (Neutestamentliche Abhandlungen XIX Band, 4 Heft), Münster, 1952, pp. 33–4.

est? [42] If Stephen wrote, as Cyprian alleges, that he was the successor of Peter, such an assertion would not have gone beyond what Cyprian had said already. We must admit that Stephen's position was very difficult. First, Cyprian had rebelled against Stephen's decision, when Stephen refused to recognize the deposition of the Spanish bishops. Next comes a peremptory demand that Stephen should depose Marcian, the Bishop of Arles. It is no exaggeration to say that Cyprian wished Stephen to follow his directions, as his predecessor Cornelius had done before. But when Stephen took to speaking in Cyprian's style, Cyprian then found his own opinions inadmissible in Stephen's mouth; he rebelled against them passionately and brought against Stephen the councils he had convoked.

Of course Stephen's own mind may well have glided from one idea into another, and sometimes taken the priority of the Roman Church to imply primacy of power. There is a world of difference between priority of authority, in the realm of witness, and primacy of power; but a change from the former to the latter was quite easy, once the idea of the Universal Church began to find favour. It came to Rome from various directions: from Carthage first of all; it next entered into the religious mind through Jewish-Christian literature; and finally found expression in Montanism. Apart from Gnostic literature, the *Didache* is the first document which contains any notion of the Universal Church; and in Montanism the idea of the Universal Church was actually put into practice. Before Catholic Rome had even come on to the scene, claiming dominion over the Universal Church, there was a Montanist Rome at Pepuza.

Even supposing that Stephen wanted to be a real pope—and I think it unlikely—his was an isolated example and had no immediate consequences. Cyprian's ecclesiological system had met opposition, even in his lifetime, and a similar ill-success attended Stephen's attempts at carrying out Cyprian's theory in practice, always supposing that he ever attempted anything of the sort. The doctrine of the Universal Church was not entirely accepted by the conscience of the pre-Nicene period. Before the beginning of the Nicene period, Rome did not hold the primacy of power. After Stephen, the Roman Church forgot about 'the Chair of Peter'

[42] Epist. LIX, 14.

for a long time. Is it not remarkable that the edicts of Gallienus, Licinius and Constantine seem unaware of the Universal Church and Rome its president? They only speak of local churches in isolation. Catholic theologians complain, with reason, that Constantine overshadowed the Bishop of Rome, and that Sylvester's pontificate was extremely insignificant.[43] To Constantine, the primacy of the Church of Rome did not exist. Further, it could not exist in *his* consciousness, because it had no legal character. And while it is true that the witness of pagan emperors and of the semi-Christian Constantine has no decisive value for us, it is scarcely likely that when these Emperors published their edicts of toleration, they could be unfamiliar with ecclesiastical organization. The decision of the Emperor Aurelian, in the case of Paul of Samosata, cannot be taken as evidence to support the primacy of the Bishop of Rome; the Emperor wanted evidence that Antioch was loyal, and saw a guarantee of this if the Bishop of Antioch were given recognition by his Italian colleagues and by the Bishop of Rome.

Now I only have one task left—to draw some conclusions from what I have been saying above. The universal ecclesiology, so prevalent in modern theology, is not really primitive. It came to replace eucharistic ecclesiology, which was the only one known in apostolic days. The foundations of universal ecclesiology were formulated for the first time by Cyprian of Carthage. With Constantine a new factor comes into the Church's life, namely the Roman Empire and the Roman Caesar. This new factor led to the predominance of universal ecclesiology in the mind of the Church. In spite of all the difference there is between these two types of ecclesiology, they agree in both accepting the idea that the whole Church must follow a single directive. For the pattern of universal ecclesiology, a unique, personal power founded on rights is a necessity. You cannot construct a universal ecclesiology without admitting the idea of primacy, nothing but the exigencies of controversy could produce anything so artificial. The question whether the primacy should belong to the Bishop of Rome or not is quite a different matter. In the pattern of eucharistic theology, power of one single bishop simply does not exist, because power based on right does not exist,

[43] A. Fliche and V. Martin, *Histoire de l'Église*, v. III, Paris, 1950, p. 36.

anyhow. But this is not saying that eucharistic ecclesiology rejects the idea that the whole church should follow a single directive; this idea springs from the basic doctrine of eucharistic ecclesiology. According to this doctrine, one of the local churches possesses the priority, which is manifested in its greater authority of witness, about events in other churches, that is, events in the Church of God in Christ, since every local church is the Church of God in Christ with all fullness. To put it otherwise, universal ecclesiology and eucharistic ecclesiology have different conceptions on the question of Church government: the first conceives this government as a matter of law and rights, and the second regards it as founded on grace. The idea of primacy, inherent in universal ecclesiology, is an idea subsequent to that of priority, just as this ecclesiology was subsequent to eucharistic ecclesiology; the concept of primacy is really the same as that of priority, only looked at from a lawyer's point of view. This explains why, in the pattern of universal ecclesiology, the primacy belongs to one of the bishops, who is at the head of the Universal Church; but in the pattern of eucharistic ecclesiology, the priority belongs to one of the local churches, and only belongs to the bishop through his church. No priority belongs to the bishop personally; he possesses it only through the local church. Priority is a concept founded on the idea of grace: it is a gift of grace, given from God to one of the local churches; and its nature is a gift of witnessing, in the name of the Church, about all that goes on within that same Church. This shows that everything happens *in* the Church, not outside it or *over* it. For this reason—that priority is a gift of witness—it cannot be fully accounted for on empirical grounds. We cannot explain why the apostle Peter occupied a special place among the apostles and had a special mission, nor why Paul was chosen by God to be the apostle to the Gentiles, nor yet why the priority, first possessed by the Church of Jerusalem, was passed over to Rome. The end of the reckoning brings us to a dilemma: we have simply to accept either priority and eucharistic ecclesiology or primacy and universal ecclesiology. By denying both we should reject the idea that the Church has a single directive—and that is an essential proposition in the Doctrine of the Church.

The Orthodox Church is absolutely right in refusing to recognize the contemporary doctrine that primacy belongs to the Bishop of Rome; however, this rightness does not lie in the numerous arguments that have been brought against primacy, but in the very fact of non-recognition. The arguments against primacy, which Orthodox school-theology offers, seem to suffer from some lack of clarity and finish. This can be explained by the fact that eucharistic ecclesiology is still alive, deep down in the Orthodox soul; but Orthodoxy on the surface is under the shadow of universal ecclesiology, and also of contemporary ecclesiastical organization. The attribute of 'catholicity,' which (in eucharistic ecclesiology) belongs to the episcopal church, has now been transferred to the autocephalous church —a unit, in fact, half political and half ecclesiastical. Naturally the episcopal church loses its catholicity and becomes a part of the autocephalous church. To this latter, alone, modern Orthodox theology ascribes the ability to be free and autonomous. Orthodox theology indeed rejects the idea of primacy on the universal scale, but it recognizes a partial primacy at the centre of every autocephalous church, a primacy belonging to the head of that church. We are concerned here with primacy, not priority, for priority implies that every local church has fullness of ecclesial *esse*. The autocephalous churches, meanwhile, have become divided and separated, for the idea of a single directive has faded since the fall of Byzantium. Ever since the second Ecumenical Council, Constantinople has been trying to bring off a Pan-Orthodox primacy, but all her attempts have failed. It would be most unwise to talk of an 'Eastern Pope,' as though the Patriarch of Constantinople set himself to copy the Bishop of Rome; and wrong whether we take an ideological or historical view. But no doubt various inner motives did impel the Patriarch of Constantinople to follow along the road to primacy, within the pattern of a universal ecclesiology. In modern times, the unity of the Orthodox Church is becoming a sort of abstract ideal, with no means of manifesting itself in the real life of the Church. Any one who regards the Pan-Orthodox or Ecumenical Council as an organ manifesting the Church's unity, is just putting things in the wrong order; consequences before foundation. In fact the Pan-Orthodox Council should be the consequence of Orthodox Church unity; it should be guided by a church or a bishop; and it cannot be a foundation for this unity.

In the long course of the struggle against the Catholic primacy of Rome, Orthodox doctrine has lost the very notion of priority.

And the Catholic Church lost sight of the idea even earlier, during its struggle for a single directive in the Church, which it had now transformed into primacy. If we take the respective positions of the two churches as they stand, there is no hope of resolving the question of primacy. We can only accept the tragedy, but with our eyes open, and without that romantic sentimentality which only adds bitterness to the everlasting discussion about primacy. 'The unity of the faith in the bond of peace.' Unity of faith still reigns within the Orthodox Church, but without union in Love; and neither exists between the Orthodox and Catholic Churches. Why is this? Surely because the mind of the Church has become unaware that the Church of God should be directed by a local church, one church among all the others. They all possess catholicity; but priority of authority, by giving witness on events in the Church's life, is something that belongs only to the church 'which presides in love.'

NICOLAS KOULOMZINE

PETER'S PLACE IN THE EARLY CHURCH

THE subject of this article is Peter's position in the early Church, according to the data which the New Testament texts provide.

Peter's history may be divided into three successive stages: (1) Peter in the primitive Church of Jerusalem (Acts 1–5), (2) Peter at the beginning of the spreading of the Gospel (Acts 6–12), (3) Peter after he left Jerusalem.

Our study of Peter's history will thus be limited to the time after Christ's ascension, and will not attempt to study his life while his Divine Master was on earth; nor give an exegesis of the Gospel texts on which his primacy has been founded.

I

The Church was formed on the day of Pentecost, at Jerusalem. There the Twelve who were the core of this Church found they must make up their minds about the function to which Christ had called and trained them. The Church of Jerusalem was, to them, the fulfilment of the Messianic Age they had been waiting for. The Book of Acts (our only source for the period) displays Peter as the *Protos* or First among the Twelve in the heart of their Church. Peter had already taken the initiative of electing the Twelfth Apostle in place of Judas (Acts 1: 15–26): he was the one of the Twelve who made the great speech of Pentecost (Acts 2: 14–36). He again, in company with John, spoke to the multitude in the temple after the lame man was healed (Acts 3: 12–26), and spoke next day before the Sanhedrin (Acts 4: 8–12). What a striking change from the Simon in the Gospel, the *man of little faith* (Matt. 14: 31), who had begun to sink in the waters, and still needed his divine Master's prayers to remain steadfast in faith at the last (Luke 22: 32)! He had plighted his faith to Jesus and denied Him thrice, and it had been hard for him to believe in the Resurrection.

In the Pentecost speech after the Holy Ghost had come down, Peter spoke in the name of the Church, and in the name of all the churches still to be established: he made, at that historic moment, the first public confession of the work of Christ, as foretold by the Scriptures; and he proclaimed His Passion, Resurrection and Ascension into glory. 'This man, being delivered up by the determinate counsel and foreknowledge of God, ye by the hand of lawless men did crucify and slay, but God raised him up' (Acts 2: 22–3). Christ whom the Scriptures promised, 'This Jesus did God raise up, whereof we all are witnesses. Being therefore by the right hand of God exalted, and having received of the Father the promise of the Holy Ghost . . .' (Acts 2: 32–3). For the first time in history the Twelve, by the mouth of Peter, confess the mystery of the Lord's being glorified, after His Passion and Resurrection: it is the first act of faith under the New Covenant. 'Let all the house of Israel therefore know assuredly that God hath made him both Lord and Christ, this Jesus whom ye crucified' (Acts 2: 36).

Long before, at Caesarea Philippi, the Twelve had not understood the mystery of their Master's sufferings and glory; and on the road to Gethsemane they had still, perhaps, not fully understood the scope of the promise assuring to them the Paraclete who would 'teach them all things' (John 14: 26). But now Peter, in the midst of the Twelve, in the Pentecost speech, before the people gathered in the temple court, proclaims the coming down of the Spirit. He alludes to Joel's prophecy 'And it shall be in the last days, saith God, I will pour forth my Spirit upon all flesh: and your sons and your daughters shall prophesy. Your young men shall see visions, and your old men shall dream dreams. Yea, and on my handmaidens, in those days, will I pour forth of my Spirit' (Joel 2: 28–9; Acts 2: 17–18). Peter, like a prophet of old, and being himself a prophet among the other prophets of the New Church, makes the solemn affirmation that Christ 'being therefore by the right hand of God exalted, and having received of the Father the promise of the Holy Ghost, hath poured forth this, which ye see and hear' (Acts 2: 33). Peter the prophet unveils the hidden meanings of the Scriptures, and reveals in them a plan conceived in the mysterious being of the Trinity. Once the Son has finished His work, the Father exalts Him, and so makes possible the descent of the Holy Ghost. By the mouth of Peter, first of the Twelve, the Church of the New Covenant comes to its first knowledge of the mystery of the Trinity, now fully revealed; so that it may become (as Peter himself will say in his epistle) the Church of the Elect 'according to the foreknowledge of God the Father, in sanctification of the Spirit, unto obedience and sprinkling of the blood of Jesus Christ' (1 Peter 1 : 2).

Immediately after the speech, Peter and the Twelve invite those present to be baptized. 'Repent ye, and be baptized, every one of you, in the name of Jesus Christ . . . and ye shall receive the gift of the Holy Ghost' (Acts 2 : 38).

Was Peter the first to take the Lord's place at the celebration of the Holy Feast? New Testament texts do not say so, but the Church's life has always centred round the Eucharist. Peter, in the midst of the Twelve and the first community at Jerusalem, was probably first in breaking the Bread.[1]

Peter is also the first thaumaturge: with John as companion, he performs the cure of the lame man (Acts 3 : 1ff.). He is specially cited among the other miracle-working apostles (Acts 5 : 12) and his shadow brings miracles to pass (Acts 5 : 15). He is also Judge (with the Twelve) in the first community at Jerusalem (the incident of Ananias and Sapphira, Acts 5). It is he who presides, with the Twelve, over the organization and administration of their communal possessions (a charge afterwards entrusted to the Seven by the Twelve, Acts 2 : 42; 4 : 34; see also 6 : 1). Finally, Peter is held first responsible to answer before the Sanhedrin (accompanied by John in Chapter 4 and the other apostles in Chapter 5). During the first period in the life of the Mother-Church of Jerusalem, the part Peter plays is obviously in the forefront.

But how can we describe this part? The word 'head' or 'chief' implies a personal power to command, but nothing of the sort is specifically set down by the texts. The word 'president' sounds wrong, something of an anachronism. The title of First Bishop must also be rejected, for this is an absolute anachronism in the first period and takes no account of the part played by the other apostles, among whom Peter is, as it were, *primus inter pares;* neither does it recognize what an entirely special and unique situation there was in the Pentecostal Church. Saint Matthew does not use any such titles (and his materials and their composition are

---

[1] cf. Nicolas Afanassieff, *The Lord's Table*, Paris, 1952 (in Russian).

H

generally traced to Jerusalem circles) : he cites Peter in the list of the Twelve Apostles (Matt. 10 : 2) with the description, or should we say title, of First; as though, apparently, it was impossible to describe his position in any better way.

But we must make clear, yet again, that Peter is first of the Twelve, first among the Twelve. The text of Acts confirms this : Peter never acts or speaks alone, but in company with the Twelve, or sometimes John. Luke, presumed author of the Book of Acts, makes this very clear, perhaps by design, in all the texts concerning Peter in the five first chapters.

But there is a further point of definition which we feel is called for. Peter had to play his part of First among the Twelve within the Pentecostal Church, and at Jerusalem. This part of Peter's was absolutely unique in history, as the Pentecostal Church was also unique in history. The Church would never again be made up so largely of eye-witnesses to the Incarnation and Glorifying of the Son, of witnesses to the coming of the Holy Ghost on Whitsunday; of witnesses to the Father's revelation in the Son and by the Spirit; of first testifiers to the Trinity. Jerusalem was also unique in having so many gifts of the Holy Ghost, given to so many. It was the pattern for future churches, and a foretaste of the heavenly Jerusalem.

It was in this Pentecostal and unrepeatable Church, that Peter stood first among the Twelve. We think that his primacy may properly be discussed, only if we regard it in that setting : i.e. in a given church, at a given (and unique) time.

The remaining part of our inquiry is to ask a threefold question : As the Church's history grew, what part belonged to Jerusalem, to the Twelve, and to Peter?

2

The first believers expected the Lord's coming from day to day : but history was bound to follow its course. We know the grand outlines of this chiefly by reading the Acts of the Apostles. Luke's method—he has been thought to be a sound historian (cf. Luke 1 : 1–4)—was to collate and arrange all his available information; documents, oral tradition and personal reminiscences. But he still could not avoid making a selection; preferring to record the events that illustrated the purpose (or purposes) of his book, stressing this or that matter as important to him. Luke's main purpose in writing the Acts was to show Theophilus—probably an influential Greek—how the Good News came to the Gentile world: how the Church of Jerusalem, at first a single body of Jews who respected the law of Moses, afterwards became the Universal Church as he knew it after A.D. 70, when his book was probably composed. Luke's purpose dictated the form of the book, which is:

(1) Chaps. 1–5. The Church of Jerusalem.
(2) Chaps. 6–12. The Good News begins to be spread in the world of the Diaspora.
(3) Chaps. 13–28. Its spreading in the Gentile world.

These may conveniently be called the first, second and third periods of first century history according to Luke's arrangement of the Acts: we will add a fourth, beginning after A.D. 70. In the first part of the Acts, as we have said above, Luke tells us about the Church of Jerusalem, the Twelve and Peter. The most important event in this period is Pentecost. In the third period, when the Good News is propagated in the Gentile world, Luke's interest turns to Paul, the apostle of the Gentiles and the great protagonist of the wider evangelism. His arrival in Rome is the logical point to end the book: the Good News, represented by Paul in person, reaches the Capital of the Empire. The second period must be regarded as a time of transition, a beginning to spread the Gospel, but mostly among the Jewish Diaspora.

Luke is a historian first, but a theologian as well. The history he writes is the history of the Church, its life and its growth. And he sees, beyond history, the Church's unity in the abiding and life-giving activity of the Holy Ghost.

Can we really say that the Church was a hierarchical structure in the first century? In the second, St. Ignatius of Antioch bears witness in his letters to the existence of local churches, each centred round one particular bishop, accompanied by presbyters, and aided by deacons. But this state of affairs is the final product of a formative period: the list of hierarchical orders had become progressively more uniform. If we speak of hierarchical structure in the Church when its history began, we are in danger of falling into anachronisms, and being forced to use inadequate terms. Yet, with all these reservations, we still think we can find, in the Acts, pieces of valuable information about the part played by Jerusalem, the

Twelve, and Peter. Luke does, of course, schematize and harmonize, unlike Paul, whose epistles are direct evidence. Luke writes later, at a time when the burning questions, between Jewish-born and Gentile-born Christians, are settled. Some Gnostical doctrines are beginning to creep into the fold, and the Church must now make sure of unity, and set its house in order. Concern to show that its development was continuous was never out of Luke's mind when he wrote Acts.

One concern is conspicuously absent in his work: he does not try to give us a complete life-picture of any character, even Peter or Paul. We should like to be told more about Peter's fate after he left Jerusalem (Acts 12: 17), and Paul's after he came to Rome. But Luke was only interested in the parts Peter or Paul played in the Church's history: that Church which, in spite of the world's indifference or enmity, even despite the weaknesses and hesitations of the Christians themselves, goes on up the royal road marked out by the feet of Christ and by the Spirit's direction.

Luke's task as a Church historian for the middle period (covering Acts 6–12), which we are now approaching, was more complicated than it was for the first period. The main subject of these chapters is the spreading of the Gospel in the Jewish world of the Diaspora. This preceded, and made possible, a further transmission of the Good News to the Gentiles proper.

According to Luke's ideas, the spreading of the Gospel outside the bounds of Jerusalem had its starting-point in the persecution which followed Stephen's martyrdom. We may take it that this persecution was provoked by the attitude taken by the 'hellenist' members of the Church of Jerusalem [2] (Acts 7: 41–53). 'And there arose on that day a great persecution against the church which was in Jerusalem; and they were all scattered abroad throughout the regions of Judaea and Samaria, except the Apostles' (Acts 8: 1). These 'scattered' Christians were, according to Luke, the first to preach the Gospel outside the walls of Jerusalem. Philip was one of them, and went to Samaria (Chapter 8) where his teaching was crowned with success; and he baptized the Ethiopian. Was Ananias

[2] The Hellenists are Jews of the Diaspora, Jewish by religion but Greek-speaking, giving their obedience to the hierarchic religious centre of Jerusalem. They often had Greek names as well as their Jewish ones (e.g. John-Mark, Saul-Paul). The early Church of Jerusalem consisted of Jewish and Jewish-hellenist converts. Cornelius (Ch. 10) will be the first Gentile to be converted.

also one of them, the Ananias who received Paul at Damascus?
We cannot tell. Were the churches visited by Peter (Acts 9:
32–43) evangelized by Christians scattered from Jerusalem?
Probably they were. One thing we can be sure of, 'They that were
scattered abroad upon the tribulation that arose about Stephen
travelled as far as Phoenicia and Cyprus and Antioch' (Acts
11: 19) first only preaching to Jews, but at Antioch to Gentiles
also (Acts 11: 19–20).

Jerusalem, where the Twelve continued to stay, does not seem
at this time to be taking the initiative in evangelization. Their part
is described by Luke: 'Now when the apostles which were at
Jerusalem heard that Samaria had received the word of God, they
sent unto them Peter and John who, when they were come down,
prayed for them, that they might receive the Holy Ghost, for as
yet He was fallen upon none of them: only they had been baptized
into the name of the Lord Jesus. Then laid they their hands on
them, and they received the Holy Ghost' (Acts 8: 14–17). The
evangelization carried out by others (not the Twelve) receives
something from Jerusalem the centre, namely, confirmation by the
laying-on of apostles' hands; so that the new communities, in
receiving the Holy Spirit, may in turn acquire fullness in their
life as churches. 'They (the churches) were edified, and walking
in the fear of the Lord, and in the comfort of the Holy Ghost, were
multiplied' (Acts 9: 31). The Twelve were not members of these
churches; only, acting in the name of Jerusalem, they gave the
Holy Spirit to them, and the new churches were born into the
graces of the Spirit, as the Mother-Church of Jerusalem was born
on the day of Pentecost.

Peter is always in the forefront among the Twelve. He goes to
Samaria, his name being paired with John's. Still more significant
is his visit to a whole list of churches (*vide* Acts 9: 32–43). This
is the period when he receives a special revelation from Christ
concerning the baptism of Cornelius, the first Gentile to come
into the Church. Luke stresses this, and gives a long and detailed
account (Acts 10: 1–11, 18).

It should be noticed, however, that Peter's part in this period
cannot be dissociated from the parts played by the Twelve, and by
Jerusalem, any more than it could be in the preceding period,
which we have already discussed. In fact it was the Twelve, still

in Jerusalem, who dispatched Peter and John to Samaria (Acts 8: 14). Again Jerusalem was the place and the Twelve were the body to which Peter reported on his activities during this period. Luke is careful to point this out: 'Now the apostles and the brethren that were in Judaea heard that the Gentiles also had received the Word of God. And when Peter was come up to Jerusalem, they that were of the circumcision contended with him' (Acts 11: 1-2), and reproached him for having eaten with Gentiles. But Peter told of the miracles that had come with Cornelius's conversion, and appeased the assembly (Acts 11: 1-18). Peter's dependence on the Twelve and on the Church of Jerusalem is thus very clearly underlined by the author of Acts. When the Gospel began to be propagated outside the bounds of Judaea, Jerusalem still kept its central place among the new churches springing up. It presided at their birth by sending apostles as representatives. The Twelve still had their seats at Jerusalem and, among them, Peter continued to occupy the first place.

But during this same period a new character steps on to the historical scene, Saul, the future apostle of the Gentiles. He is first mentioned in the account of Stephen's martyrdom: then he has a vision of Christ while Peter is going round visiting the churches. In the times that followed, Paul never lost the conviction that he had received his election from Christ himself, and not from men. He begins his epistle to the Galatians by saying 'Paul, an apostle not from men, neither through man, but through Jesus Christ, and God the Father, who raised him from the dead' (Gal. 1: 1). He returns to the point; 'For I make known to you, brethren, as touching the gospel which was preached by me, that it is not after man. For neither did I receive it from man, nor was I taught it, but it came to me through revelation of Jesus Christ' (Gal. 1: 11-12).[3] Christ's revelation dispensed him from receiving his apostolic power from the hands of the Twelve of Jerusalem: in the same epistle, we read 'But when it was the good pleasure of God, who separated me, even from my mother's womb, and called me through his grace, to reveal his Son in me, that I might preach him among the Gentiles: immediately I conferred not with flesh and blood,

---

[3] See also 1 Cor. 9:1; 5: 5-8, and the three accounts of Paul's conversion in Acts 9, 22 and 26.

neither went I up to Jerusalem, to them which were apostles before me; but I went away into Arabia; and again I returned unto Damascus' (Gal. 1: 15–17). Christ Himself makes Paul His Apostle.

But Luke, in his concern to show the Church in proper unity and continuity, takes careful note that Paul did not remain a stranger to the community of Jerusalem. The chronological order of his action after being baptized is difficult for us to grasp entirely, because it is difficult to co-ordinate Luke's data with those of Paul himself. Luke tells us that Paul, once converted, turns his eyes towards the centre, Jerusalem, where he is presented by Barnabas to the Twelve (Acts 9: 26ff). But Paul says in clear terms that he only appeared at Jerusalem three years later, and then paid a visit to Peter alone, of the Twelve, and stayed no longer than fifteen days (Gal. 1: 18). This visit of Paul's to Jerusalem was certainly not an act of submission on his part, but much more like an act of communion with the mother-church.

The birth of the Church of Antioch, which was founded by fugitives from the persecution at Jerusalem, is another important event at the end of this period. It was there that the Good News was proclaimed to the Gentiles for the first time, after Cornelius was converted (Acts 11: 19–21). Antioch was called to be the centre from which Paul would set out to conquer the Gentile world.

Jerusalem was perturbed again, as it had been perturbed when Peter returned after the conversion of Cornelius (Acts 11: 1). The man who was sent to the new church this time was not one of the twelve, but a member of their congregation, Barnabas, 'a good man, full of the Holy Ghost and of faith' (Acts 11: 24), 'who, when he was come, and had seen the grace of God, was glad; and he exhorted them all, that with purpose of heart they would cleave unto the Lord' (Acts 11: 23). Barnabas was content to observe the facts, and encourage the faithful. One of his first concerns was to find Paul, who had just then retired to Tarsus. Although Jerusalem had felt perturbed about what was going on at Antioch, one does have the impression that the Church of Antioch was beginning to feel more independent in its relations with Jerusalem. A personal confirmation by one of the Twelve was no longer the form.

A new persecution marks the end of this period, that of Herod Agrippa (Acts 12: 1). One of the Twelve, James, the brother of

John and son of Zebedee, is the first victim.[4] From this time onwards there is no further mention made in the New Testament of a permanent college of the Twelve; after the martyrdom of James, son of Zebedee, they did not proceed to elect a Twelfth, as they had done after the treachery and death of Judas. From now on, throughout the New Testament, the Twelve (or Eleven) are mentioned only twice: once in 1 Cor. 15: 5, in connection with the appearances of the risen Christ; and a second time in the Apocalypse where it speaks of Jerusalem to come (Rev. 21: 14).

During this persecution, Peter himself was imprisoned; after his miraculous deliverance, he visited the house of Mary, mother of John Mark, and then withdrew from Jerusalem. The Acts tell us that Peter departed and went 'to another place'—εἰς ἕτερον τόπον (Acts 12: 17). 'Other,' we take it, means 'other than Jerusalem.'

To conclude our examination of this second period in the Church's life, we feel that we may fairly state as follows: Jerusalem still presided at the birth of the first local churches outside the territory of Judaea; it remained the hierarchic centre for these churches, to a degree, that is, so long as the Twelve continued in their seats. Peter always held first place among the Twelve, but the parat he played in the Church was still bound up with the part of the Twelve and Jerusalem. We have observed, though, that the birth of the Church of Antioch, and the coming of Paul, already signify that a new period is about to begin.

3

We come now to the third historical period, which begins with Herod's persecution, and to its chief results, the death of James, the son of Zebedee, and Peter's departure; it ends with the destruction of Jerusalem.

Luke, in the Book of Acts, is still our principal source of information (Ch. 13–28). His interest is focused on Paul, almost exclusively: and he ends his story when Paul reaches Rome, an event that marked (or so he thought) the unmistakable lodgement of Christianity in the Gentile world.

The epistles that were written during this third period fill in and

[4] Not to be confused with James son of Alpheus, one of the Twelve, nor with James the brother of the Lord, of whom we will presently have more to say.

clarify the historical picture given by Luke. (Paul most of all, but Peter, Jude and James contribute in a smaller way.)

We have been trying to show that Peter's primacy is supported by New Testament witness, so long as his part lay in the midst of the Twelve at Jerusalem, and within the Pentecostal Church: there is still support for it in the second, or intermediate period, in so far as the Twelve still retain their seat at Jerusalem. Now we must try to see whether this state of affairs continued in existence during the third period; and we must study the New Testament data on three subjects in turn—Peter, the Twelve, and the Church of Jerusalem.

A. THE TRAVELLING MINISTRY OF PETER AND PAUL

Paul's activities are the better-known to us, and may be briefly outlined as follows. He makes three missionary journeys, as Luke relates in Acts. After the first, there is the Antioch incident which sets Paul against Peter (Acts 15: 1–3 and Gal. 2: 11–14); there is also the Council of Jerusalem (Acts 15: 4–35 and Gal. 2: 1–10). After his third journey, Paul is arrested at Jerusalem; then, for nearly two years, he remained at Caesarea in chains (Acts 21: 17–24). When Festus took the place of Felix and became Procurator of Judaea, Paul appealed to Caesar for judgment and got transferred to Rome (Acts 25).

We will take it that Paul wrote the two epistles to the Thessalonians during his second journey; and that his four great epistles[5] were dispatched in the course of his third journey: after his transfer to Rome and during his two years captivity (Acts 28: 30–1) he wrote the four 'epistles of the captivity.'[6] Considering the historical data and the new geographical allusions we find in Paul's so-called 'pastoral' epistles,[7] we may allow ourselves to suppose that Paul made at least one other missionary journey. He would die a martyr at Rome, after a second arrest. If it is ever possible to say that the Epistle to the Hebrews was written under the personal inspiration of Paul, then its composition must be dated to the very end of the Apostle's life.[8]

[5] In order of their appearance in the New Testament, the epistles to the Romans, 1 Corinthians, 2 Corinthians and Galatians.

[6] Again in order of New Testament place, Ephesians, Philippians, Colossians and Philemon.

[7] 1 Timothy, 2 Timothy and Titus.

[8] For details, see Bishop Cassian, *Le Christ et la première generation des chrétiens,* Paris, 1950 (in Russian).

We have much less good information about Peter's fate after he left Jerusalem (Acts 12: 17). Local tradition in the Church of Rome strongly asserted that Peter had died a martyr at Rome. But the New Testament gives us only one indication of his presence in the capital city, and that is the mention of Babylon as the place from which the first Epistle had been sent out. 'She (the Church) which is at Babylon, elect together with you, saluteth you' (1 Pet. 5: 13). This precious fragment of information supports the tradition, but it only concerns the end of Peter's life; the epistle was probably sent out in the later sixties, possibly after the death of Paul.[9]

Where did Peter go to after he left Jerusalem? (Acts 12: 17). The New Testament text does not tell us. It is not said that Peter appeared at Rome straight away. On the contrary: we find him next at Antioch, at the time of the controversy when he and Paul were set against each other; and Paul was the one who reported the fact in Gal. 2: 11–14.

We find Peter back at Jerusalem for the Council, when he defended Paul and Barnabas, who were in trouble with their Jerusalem brethren, so zealous for the law of Moses. We shall have more to say about this council latter on.

We are told that Peter had disciples within the Church of Corinth (1 Cor. 1: 12; 3: 22); but this cannot be taken to prove that Peter had made a personal visit to Corinth.

Peter was not at Rome during Paul's third journey; for the Epistle to the Romans, so rich in greetings to Paul's many friends at Rome, does not mention Peter's name at all. There is a further valuable detail to add from the same Epistle: Paul apologizes for not having visited the Romans; he wanted to, but he felt scruples against building 'upon another man's foundation' (Rom. 15: 20). If Peter had been the 'other man,' Paul's pen would have written the Great Apostle's name almost unbidden; for it would have strengthened his argument.

When Paul came to Rome in chains later on, Luke does not mention Peter's name in the list of 'brethren' who went to meet him. And the omission is significant, for it is supported by the silence of the captivity epistles, written by Paul from Rome in the course of the next two years.

[9] Cassian, ibid., p. 291.

In the period before Paul's death, Peter's name is again un-
mentioned, not only in the pastoral epistles, but also—and this
means more—in the Epistle to the Hebrews, written at Rome in
the name of 'they of Italy' (Heb. 13: 24).

After that, there is only the evidence of 1 Peter 5: 1, which
concerns Peter's life later on, when Paul had perhaps departed to
another world.

The general rules say that arguments *e silentio* are not sufficient
to provide a positive datum. But in Peter's case, the omissions we
spoke of may be of some value. One conclusion seems to be
obvious; Peter's work, after he left Jerusalem (Acts 12: 17), was
not tied any more to a single place on the map, or a special
church.

Jerusalem anyhow cannot have been the permanent seat of
Peter, since James, the brother of the Lord, is always the one
called leader of the church, once Peter has departed. As for
Antioch—the church there was certainly not of Peter's foundation
(Acts 11: 19–30). Neither was he one of the group that appointed
Paul and Barnabas to go on their first mission (Acts 13: 1–3).
Peter must have really been at Antioch, or Paul would not have
emphatically said so (cf. controversy with Peter, Gal. 2: 11–14):
but Acts never refers to Peter being at Antioch, so it must have
been a passing visit.

There are two possible hypotheses for Peter's presence at Rome:
either he went there often, and was often away, or else he arrived
very late (perhaps after the death of Paul). In either case, it is an
impossibility that Peter had a permanent seat at Rome.

Everything leads us to think that Peter's ministry was peripatetic. His work did not install him in the headship of any given
local church. Did he join the *collegium* of elders in the various
churches that he was led to visit? When he had come to Rome, he
called himself 'fellow-elder' (1 Peter 5: 1). These are words of
shining humility when the great Apostle speaks them; but surely
they prove just the opposite—that his real title as Christ's Apostle
placed him in a much higher position than a mere elder in a local
church.

We believe that this is a reasonable way to talk about the
apostle Peter; but in Paul's case it is self-evident. We need not
bother to give examples to show that the Apostle of the Gentiles

claimed no part in the local hierarchies of any churches which he founded. As an Apostle of Christ, his ministry was by nature a travelling ministry, and set him above the several churches. He laid his hands upon the elders of these churches, sent letters to some of them, gave them counsels and, indeed, commands, and reserved to himself the right to excommunicate. Peter had acted in this way during the second period, of which we know more and have spoken already. He paid visits to churches that he did not belong to and, like Paul, he had the right to excommunicate (Simon Magus in Samaria, Acts 8). Surely his apostolic activity after Acts 12 : 17 continued on the same lines.

B. THE APOSTLES. THE TWELVE

Peter, one of the Twelve and first of the Twelve at Jerusalem, afterwards had to fulfil his mission as an Apostle of Christ. So the two terms 'Apostle' and 'Twelve' deserve our special consideration.

All four evangelists very frequently use the word $\mu\alpha\theta\eta\tau\dot{\eta}s$ for the disciples of Christ: and $\delta\dot{\omega}\delta\epsilon\kappa\alpha$ for that inner circle, the Twelve. But the word $\dot{\alpha}\pi\dot{o}\sigma\tau o\lambda os$ is very rarely used. John's Gospel uses it only once, and to mean envoy, not Apostle; the noun is common, not the title properly given to the Twelve. 'A servant is not greater than his lord, neither one that is sent ($\dot{\alpha}\pi\dot{o}\sigma\tau o\lambda os$) greater than he that sent him' (13 : 16). In Mark, too, the word appears once only: when the Twelve come back from the mission on which Christ had sent them: 'And the Apostles gather themselves together unto Jesus' (6 : 30)—but it can equally well be translated 'And they that were sent . . .' meaning those whom Christ had sent on a mission. In the Gospel according to Matthew *apostle* occurs once alone, and clearly designates the Twelve by their title: 'Now the names of the Twelve Apostles are these' (10 : 2). So in all the three Gospels quoted, there is no more than one (or at most two) texts where *apostle* is used to name the Twelve by their proper title. We should also notice at once how often the verb $\dot{\alpha}\pi o\sigma\tau\acute{\epsilon}\lambda\lambda\omega$ recurs in the Gospels, and how much evidence there is of the disciples being sent on missions.

Luke's Gospel, on the other hand, uses $\dot{\alpha}\pi\dot{o}\sigma\tau o\lambda os$ several times, five of which apply clearly and unequivocally to the Twelve (6 : 13; 9 : 10; 17 : 5; 22 : 14; 24 : 10); and once it is used in a more general sense (11 : 49).

The word hardly appears at all in the first two Gospels, which were composed before A.D. 70, and whose source-material was drawn, directly or indirectly, from the stock teaching for catechumens at Jerusalem. This leaves us free to suppose that in the early history of the Church, the word *Apostle* was not commonly used to describe the Twelve.

In Luke's Gospel, however (generally thought to have been written after A.D. 70), the word is there, a proof, surely, that it became the proper description of the Twelve at some particular date—probably in the third period. The Book of Acts gives confirmation to this hypothesis; Luke keeps the word *Apostle* almost exclusively to describe the Twelve. And it is Luke alone who thinks it needful to explain in his Gospel that the title *Apostle* was bestowed on the Twelve by Christ in person. After giving a list of the Twelve, Luke goes on to say 'twelve, whom also he named Apostles' (6: 13). Matthew and Mark forgot to put this in, but the explanation is easy: the substance of both Gospels was based on the instruction given to catechumens at Jerusalem in those early days when they still spoke of the disciples, the twelve disciples, and the Twelve. The additional detail, given by Luke, points to a time when the Twelve have already become commonly named Apostles, and when they found themselves ready to enact the part for which Christ had trained them.

The Pauline writings provide us with additional information, all of which seems to strengthen our theory. Of course the great Apostle of the Gentiles had a striking personality, which put him in a different position from the group of the Twelve Apostles; but the way he himself uses the word Apostle is indirect evidence of how it was used in the third historical period, which is our present concern. Paul does not regularly entitle himself Apostle (or rather Apostle of Christ) before his third missionary journey: from then onwards, it comes in the headings of all his Epistles (except Hebrews, which does not carry the author's name or—*a fortiori*—his title, and is certainly not Paul's handiwork). In the text of one of Paul's first two Epistles, which were written as early as the second journey, there is some ground (1 Thess. 2: 6–7) for thinking that the name Apostle was used to designate Paul, Sylvanus and Timothy, since their names are all in the heading. Osty translates 'Nous aurions pu nous donner de l'importance en notre qualitié d'Apôtre du Christ.' [New translation: 'We could have made our weight felt as Apostles of Christ.']

'Apostle of Christ' is the description Paul gives himself systematically from his third journey on, and as he writes, it gradually begins to emerge as a title that ranks him with the Twelve: but he called them such names as 'the chiefest Apostles' (2 Cor. 11: 5; 12: 11) or 'the Apostles that were before me' (Gal. 1: 17). In the mass of Pauline texts, again, the word *Apostle* is not confined to the Twelve, or to Paul. We can read him speaking of 'apostles of the churches' (2 Cor. 8: 23). And who, incidentally, were 'all the apostles' to whom the risen Christ appeared? (1 Cor. 15: 7). Does 'us the apostles' in 1 Cor. 4: 9 mean Paul and Apollos? The text of Romans 16: 7 is not very clear in meaning, but the word *Apostle* may be used there to describe other men than the Twelve. And Paul evidently did not rank the Twelve alone with the prophets and teachers, in passages like Eph. 2: 20; 3: 5; 4: 11.

We need not work out the meaning of *apostle* in detail: we are content to assume, on the credit of the Pauline writings, that this name was gradually given to a wider circle than the Twelve; it happened in the third period. When the Good News began to spread outside Jerusalem and beyond Judaea, it is probable that Jerusalem first, and other churches later, sent out missionaries— envoys, apostles. And it was probably not until the Twelve began to go away from Jerusalem, to become missionaries too, that their position as apostles or envoys took shape. Then was the time for them to carry out their divine Master's injunction, and preach even to the ends of the earth.

'The Twelve' is a term which gradually fades out of the New Testament vocabulary, as we can all observe. After Herod's persecution, the death of one of the Twelve, and Peter's departure (Acts 12), the question of keeping up a permanent *collegium* of Twelve is never raised again, anywhere in the New Testament. Luke has no new story about a second election of a Twelfth. As we said before, from this point onwards, the Twelve (or Eleven) are only mentioned twice more in the whole New Testament: first by Paul, when he recounts the appearance of Christ risen (1 Cor. 15: 5); and once more in John's Apocalypse (21: 14) telling of the heavenly Jerusalem. The Twelve, as a *collegium,* vanish from the scene of Church history from the third period onwards. The

New Testament text only mentions Peter's going away (Acts 12 : 17), and the death of James, son of Zebedee. There are no texts that tell us when the Ten others left Jerusalem, what roads they took, nor are we told the story of their apostolic lives (apart from what little information we can glean about John).

The only point we can make with confidence is this : they became Apostles, and that among other apostles, whom the churches had sent on missions.

With regard to the fourth period (after A.D. 70), Luke's writings show a tendency to keep the title of Apostles for the Twelve alone : this is clear in the Gospel, and borne out by Acts, where the word is used frequently and almost always to describe the Twelve. There is one notable exception in Chapter 14, where it is applied to Paul and Barnabas (in verse 4 and perhaps also verse 14 where the word is ill-evidenced). This exception again supports my assertion that the field of those qualified to be Apostles had spread, in the third period, to a wider circle than the Twelve; on the other hand, Luke generally keeps this title for the Twelve, which may be evidence of a similarly restrictive tendency, general in the Church during the fourth period (after A.D. 70). The few uses of ἀπόστολος found in New Testament texts of the fourth period rather confirm this,[10] though we cannot say that every one had such a marked tendency as St. Luke to keep this title for the Twelve.

C. JERUSALEM IN THE THIRD PERIOD

When Peter has gone away (Acts 12 : 17) James is the one always mentioned as head of the Church of Jerusalem. Traditional exegesis in the Eastern Church has always agreed that this James was the 'brother of the Lord,' and not James, son of Alpheus, one of the Twelve. In the West both persons were confusedly called James the Less, as opposed to James the Greater, son of Zebedee, who died a martyr's death under Herod (Acts 12 : 2). To-day some respectable Western exegetes have come over to the view that James, the leader of the congregation at Jerusalem, is indeed the 'brother of the Lord,' and by no means James, son of Alpheus, whose fate is as little known to us as that of most of the Twelve.

During our Lord's life on earth, his 'brethren' remained sceptical. Afterwards, James is listed by Paul in the number of those to whom

[10] 1 Peter 1 : 1; 2 Peter 1 : 1; 3 : 2; Jude 17; Rev. 2 : 2; 18 : 20; 21 : 14.

the risen Christ appeared (1 Cor. 15: 7). The brethren of the Lord are mentioned in Luke beside the Twelve, before Pentecost (Acts 1: 14). Finally, James is mentioned by Paul after his first visit to Jerusalem (Gal. 1: 19) as an important member of the congregation, even before Peter went away.

Peter sent particularly to James, to announce his departure (Acts 12: 17). Henceforward he is always referred to as leader of the Church of Jerusalem, and these references are constant and numerous. One New Testament text seems to call him an Apostle: Gal. 1: 19, 'But other of the Apostles saw I none, save James the Lord's brother,' says Paul. The text can also be translated 'but only James the Lord's brother,' as Osty has noticed; and the French 'Bible of Jerusalem' in fact adopts this translation; which means not including him in the list of the Apostles. There are two other New Testament texts which also seem to exclude James from the rank of Apostle: 1 Cor. 9: 5; 15: 7. As we said before, the apostolic ministry was peripatetic; but James's position at Jerusalem was naturally bound up with one particular local church. He was given a place above the other presbyters of that church, and acted as their Superior (Acts 21: 18). Proof that the presbyters existed, in the third period, is abundantly given by Paul and by Luke. The word $\epsilon\pi\iota\sigma\kappa\sigma\pi\sigma\varsigma$ was also used ,in this period, to describe a presbyter, as a careful reading of some texts will show (viz. Acts 15: 17 and 20: 28 put together, also Titus 1: 5–9). Whether there were bishops, in the later sense of the word, as heads of local churches, is a question we have no evidence for in the third period. But the part that James played at Jerusalem, when Peter had gone, is surely very comparable with the part bishops were to play later on: a lifelong and continuous place as leader of a local church, with a group of presbyters in support. James may not have been called a bishop, but he was in fact the first monarchical bishop of a local church.

A further question must now be tackled: what was Jerusalem's position *vis-à-vis* the other churches? We have already tried to show that it went on being the hierarchical centre, all through the second period; and that the new congregations felt their dependent relationship towards the mother-church. This authority belonged to Jerusalem because the Twelve were there, and the first persecution did not dislodge them: an authority wielded by the Twelve with Peter still the first of the Twelve. But as we have already pointed out, the end of this period saw the birth of the Church of Antioch and Paul's appearance on the scene; both of which are signs that a new period is beginning.

The history really takes a new slant in the third period, after Peter's departure. Paul and Barnabas, after staying awhile at Antioch, are sent on a mission, and Jerusalem has no part in sending them. Although Luke begins by mentioning the close ties between Antioch and Jerusalem later, life at Antioch seems to go on by itself, and be independent of Jerusalem. At the very time when Jerusalem was built up as a local church with James at the helm, the Church of Antioch also began its own life as an independent local church; but it had no sovereign bishop then, as far as we know, to govern it; churches founded by Paul generally had not either. Formerly, Peter and John were sent on a mission by the Twelve of Jerusalem; now, Paul and Barnabas are also sent on a mission, by the Church of Antioch (or rather by various prophets and teachers, possibly from Jerusalem but then settled at Antioch). While Paul and Barnabas were still on this first missionary journey, Luke described them as apostles, as we noted above; a word which in Luke's vocabulary is confined to the Twelve of Jerusalem, apart from this passage (*vide* Acts 14 : 4 and perhaps 14, where the text is uncertain). Jerusalem is still, to Christian hearts and memories, the mother-church, the place of Pentecost and the first to send out missionaries. But after Peter left, and James, son of Zebedee, died, the Twelve ceased to exercise their authority from Jerusalem. The community led by James, the brother of the Lord, was the earliest, chronologically, of all the local churches to be revered by all, but without any direct authority over the other churches : these, as the first century went on, were gradually going to follow the new pattern, and turn into local churches each with one sovereign bishop as leader.

The story of the Council of Jerusalem (Acts 15 and Gal. 2) is of special interest to us, for the information it gives on Jerusalem's position, and on the part her church played in the third period. Paul and Barnabas, once they were back from their first mission and had preached to the Gentiles, naturally came back to Antioch, whose mission had been laid upon them. And there, at Antioch, a serious controversy took place between Paul and Barnabas on

I

one side, and 'certain men who came down from Judaea,' members of James's congregation, on the other: the subject being whether it was obligatory, for Gentiles coming into the church, to make a previous submission to the Law of Moses; especially, need they be circumcised? (Acts 14: 27–15: 2). This is no longer the Church of Jerusalem saying, by the voices of the Twelve, that it is perturbed about what Paul and Barnabas had done, as they had been perturbed in the second period by Peter's actions after the conversion of Cornelius (Acts 11: 1), or by the preaching to the Greeks at Antioch (Acts 11: 19–26). The issue was raised by zealots for the law of Moses, not by the Church of Jerusalem as such. We may even suppose that this controversy was the background on which Peter's opposition to Paul at Antioch should be placed [11] (Gal. 2: 11–14). In order to end the discussion and stop the disturbance that the judaizing agitators made, 'it was resolved' (we could also translate '*they* resolved') to present their case at Jerusalem before the apostles and presbyters (Acts 15: 2). Now, the call does not come from Jerusalem: Antioch, the Church of Antioch, decides. The decision was not taken on the grounds of Jerusalem's rights, or authority as a hierarchic centre. It was a difficult time and the Council's decision was needed to decide the Church's future; so they decided to go together to the place where the Holy Ghost came down and founded the church; and so the Council dared to conclude with 'it seemed good to the Holy Ghost and to us . . .'

New troubles arose at Jerusalem, made by Christians brought up with a background of Pharisaism (Acts 15: 5–6): further vociferous charges were brought against Paul and Barnabas. The Apostles and presbyters met together to sift things out (Acts 15: 6). Peter took the same side as Paul and Barnabas. When the discussion was at its height—and it seems to have been stormy—he rose to speak. Peter was first to intervene, with authority too, but his action was not based on his present position in the Church. He explained it by referring to his own past: 'Brethren, ye know how that a good while ago God made choice among you, that by my mouth the Gentiles should hear the word of the Gospel and believe' (Acts 15: 7); this probably alludes to the baptism of

---

[11] We are supposing that Gal. 2: 11–14 should be read, not as a sequel to the first part of the epistle, which is historical in character, but as a beginning of Paul's argument. This is not the only hypothesis possible.

Cornelius's household, which happened in such special circumstances that Peter had to explain them to the Twelve at Jerusalem. 'And God, which knoweth the heart, bare them witness, giving them the Holy Ghost, even as he did unto us: and he made no distinction between us and them, cleansing their hearts by faith. Now therefore why tempt ye God, that ye should put a yoke upon the neck of the disciples, which neither our fathers nor we were able to bear? But we believe that we shall be saved through the grace of the Lord Jesus, in like manner as they' (Acts 15: 8–11).

'Then all the multitude kept silence' (Acts 15: 12). Peter's intervention had restored peace. Paul and Barnabas were able to take a turn in speaking and 'rehearsing what signs and wonders God had wrought among the Gentiles by them' (Acts 15: 12).

When the assembly again held their peace, it was James's turn to have the last word. He repeats Peter's arguments in justification of Paul and Barnabas, and supports them by a quotation from Isaiah: thus bringing the debate to a specially solemn conclusion—official would be the modern word. 'Wherefore my judgement is, that we trouble not them which from among the Gentiles turn to God' (Acts 15: 19). Peter's intervention may seem to have carried more weight in the meeting, but the presidency of the assembly belonged to James alone. Peter had authority to bear witness of past events, so he took on himself the main part in defence of Paul and Barnabas; but James had the summing-up, and James, in the first person, pronounced the final judgment. This part was his by right of place, for he was inside the local church of Jerusalem and placed at its head (with the presbyters supporting him), ever since Peter had gone (Acts 12: 17). Because James was thus placed at Jerusalem, any assembly that met there would have him as president, in spite of personalities like Peter having great authority. The fact that James did so preside, at the Council of Jerusalem and afterwards, did not in any way weaken the supremacy of the Apostles over the churches they had already founded. The text of the letter to 'the brethren which are of the Gentiles' (Acts 15: 23–9) in Antioch, Syria and Cilicia, was not signed by James, whose writ ran in Jerusalem alone; the letter was from the Apostles and presbyters.

There is an echo of this meeting to be found in Paul. Galatians 2: 1–10 is generally considered to be a parallel to

Acts 15. Paul's style of reporting events is quite different; but, after all, Luke wrote as a Church historian, whereas Paul's report is thrown off, in the course of a fervent defence against the judaizing agitators in Galatia. Paul makes a point of declaring that he went up to Jerusalem because he had received a revelation: this means, in the context, that he was not ordered to go by the 'men of repute' (Gal. 2: 2). Paul continues in Gal. 2: 6–10. 'But from those who were reputed to be somewhat (whatsoever they were, maketh no matter to me; God accepteth not man's person) —they, I say, who were of repute imparted nothing to me; but contrariwise, when they saw that I had been intrusted with the gospel of the uncircumcision, even as Peter with the gospel of the circumcision—for he that wrought for Peter unto the apostleship of the circumcision, wrought for me also unto the Gentiles; and when they perceived the grace that was given unto me, James and Cephas and John, they who were reputed to be pillars, gave to me and Barnabas the right hands of fellowship, that we should go unto the Gentiles, and they unto the circumcision; only they would that we should remember the poor; which very thing I was also zealous to do.' The circumstances under which the two accounts were composed were so different that they explain some of the discordances. Their agreement, on more points than one, seems worthy of our interest: in both, Jerusalem takes no initial step in convoking the assembly; the Apostle Paul makes no submission to the authority of Jerusalem: equal rights are confirmed for Paul on his side and the 'pillars' on theirs; and James is first to be named in the list of 'pillars' when Paul has met them at Jerusalem. The two accounts are strikingly different in character, but they agree about the essential facts, for the purposes of the present inquiry.[12]

During his third journey Paul certainly had the poor people of Jerusalem in his heart, not to be forgotten, and he organized collections for their benefit. Luke mentions this several times, and so

---

[12] It needs to be observed that Luke's account of the Council of Jerusalem, in a quite special way, has attracted criticism even from the milder school. Without describing this criticism in detail, let us only remark that it is not an impossible supposition to say: Luke, who tended to harmonize and systematize, may have mixed two distinct events into one account: (1) a Council in the second period to discuss the Gentiles, with Peter presiding, and (2) a decision made by James inside the Church of Jerusalem at a later date, which Paul would not have known about until he visited Jerusalem for the last time. If we accept this possibility, our argument will gain in strength.

does Paul himself. But, here again, this is not easily seen as Paul making an act of submission to Jerusalem. On the contrary, the natural thing to think, surely, is that Paul, who was the Apostle of the Gentiles, but himself a Jew, had a heartfelt desire to work for the unity of the Christian world.

This analysis of the Church of Jerusalem, and its position during the third period, needs a few words in conclusion. We believe we are now justified in stating that the Church of Jerusalem no longer stood for a centre or seat of authority to the Universal Church. It had turned into the first organized local church, under the authority of James, the 'brother' of the Lord, who was honoured later by Orthodox tradition as first Bishop of Jerusalem.

In studying this third period in the history of the primitive Church, we have tried to show successively: (a) that Peter's ministry, after he left Jerusalem, was a roving ministry like that of Paul, and did not bind Peter to any of the local churches he may have founded or visited; (b) the role of the Twelve as a *collegium* of twelve was limited in time to the first and second periods; (c) in the third period, Jerusalem had lost the position of being the hierarchical centre, and had become a local church among the rest of the local churches.

At Jerusalem, then, Peter's primacy, which we began by considering, was a primacy within the Twelve, tied to the presence of the Twelve and the birth of the Pentecostal Church. Peter's primacy, taken thus, is tied to a particular role, and to fixed historical conditions of a unique kind: this view finds wide support in the New Testament writings, as the beginning of our essay shows.

But as the historical conditions changed, and Peter went away from Jerusalem, he no longer figured as one of the Twelve; he became a roving Apostle. The Twelve no longer formed a *collegium* at Jerusalem, so the place then lost its position as hierarchical centre. Given these new historical conditions, is it still possible to speak of the primacy of Peter? The New Testament texts in no way show that it is.

This short study of Peter's place in the Church does not claim, of course, to have exhausted the subject of Peter's primacy in its entirety. But the Gospel texts, generally used as a basis for such discussion, are lighted up by being read in the light of the Great Apostle's life-history.

For Peter's actions after the Ascension give us a means to discover the real meaning of the words that Christ had spoken to him. Jerusalem is the place where Peter stands forth, in the Pentecostal Church and surrounded by the Twelve (he is never dissociated from them in the Gospels); here he first showed that he could be a Rock, Rock of the Church, as Christ called him when He said, 'Thou art Peter, and on this rock I will build my Church' (Matt. 16: 18). At Jerusalem, again, Peter was to show a faith that did not fail, and acted out Christ's promise, 'Thou then, when thou hast turned again, stablish thy brethren' (Luke 22: 32). And, still at Jerusalem, Peter became the Shepherd of the Church and carried out Christ's injunction, 'Feed my lambs, feed my sheep' (John 21: 15–17).

The Gospel of the Church of Jerusalem, St. Matthew's, is furthermore the Gospel which underlines Peter's primacy, and places him apart in the list of the Twelve (Matt. 10: 2); quoting the solemn word of Christ, 'Thou art Peter, and on this rock I will build my Church' (Matt. 16: 18).